Voltaire and The Orphan of China

伏尔泰与《中国孤儿》

李志远 著

Translated by Ego

五洲传播出版社
China Intercontinental Press

图书在版编目（CIP）数据

伏尔泰与《中国孤儿》：汉英对照 / 李志远著；译谷译. —北京：五洲传播出版社，2010.1
ISBN 978-7-5085-1711-7

I.①伏... II.①李...②译... III.①戏剧文学－文化交流－文化史－中国、西方国家－18世纪－汉、英 IV.①J809.249

中国版本图书馆CIP数据核字（2009）第192510号

中外文化交流故事丛书（Roads to the World）

总 策 划：	许 琳
策　　划：	马箭飞　孙文正　王锦红
顾　　问：	赵启正　沈锡麟　潘 岳
	周黎明（美）李 莎（加）威廉·林赛（英）
出 版 人：	荆孝敏　邓锦辉
编 著 者：	李志远
翻　　译：	译谷
项目统筹：	邓锦辉
责任编辑：	覃田甜
设计指导：	田 林
封面绘画：	李 骐
设计制作：	北京原色印象文化艺术中心
图　　片：	FOTOE CFP

伏尔泰与《中国孤儿》
Voltaire and *The Orphan of China*

出版发行　五洲传播出版社（北京市海淀区北小马厂6号 邮编：100038）
电　　话　8610-58891281（发行部）
网　　址　http://www.cicc.org.cn
承 印 者　北京外文印务有限公司
版　　次　2010年1月第1版第1次印刷
开　　本　720×965毫米 1/16
印　　张　11
定　　价　80.00元

Contents 目 录

Foreword *4*

I. "The Orphan" Taken to Europe *8*

II. The Story of "The Orphan of Zhao" *38*

III. *The Orphan of China* by Voltaire *80*

IV. The Appeal of *The Orphan of Zhao* in Europe *122*

前 言 *6*

1. "孤儿"被带到欧洲 *9*

2. "赵氏孤儿"的故事 *39*

3. 伏尔泰的《中国孤儿》 *81*

4. 《赵氏孤儿》在欧洲的魅力 *123*

FOREWORD

It has been a long and exciting history of tremendous cultural exchange between China and other countries. In terms of culture, economy, ideology, and personnel, these exchanges between China and other countries can be dated back to the times of Qin and Han dynasties—directly or indirectly, by land or sea. The long-term and multi-faceted cultural exchange helps the world to understand more about China and the rest of the world, enriching the common wealth of mankind—both materially and spiritually.

The book series entitled *Roads to the World* offers the most splendid stories in the entire history of Sino-foreign cultural exchange. We hereby offer them to foreign students learning the Chinese language, and to foreign readers who have a keen interest in Chinese culture. These stories depict important personalities, events, and phenomena in various fields of cultural exchange between China and other nations, and among different peoples. By reading the books, you may understand China and Chinese civilization profoundly, and the close link between Chinese civilization and other civilizations of the world. The books highlight the efforts and contributions of Chinese people and Chinese civilization in the world's cultural interchange. They reflect mankind's common spiritual pursuit and the orientation of values.

This book is a historical record of how *The Orphan of Zhao* written by Ji Junxiang, a playwright of the Yuan Dynasty of China, was adapted into *The Orphan of China* by Voltaire. Since then, this Chinese tragedy had been repeatedly translated, reviewed and adapted by different countries, creating the "craze for *The Orphan of Zhao*" across Europe in the mid-18th century. The "China fever," which emerged in Europe at the end of 17th century, also reached its climax at that time.

前　言

中国与其他国家、民族之间的文化交流具有悠久而曲折的历史。在中国与外国之间，通过间接的和直接的、陆路的和海路的、有形的和无形的多种渠道，各种文化、经济、思想、人员方面的交流，可以上溯至秦汉时代，下及于当今社会。长期的、多方面的交流，增进了中国与其他国家、民族之间的了解，使人类的共同财富（物质的和精神的）更加丰富。

中外文化交流故事丛书（Roads to the World）的宗旨，是从中外文化交流的历史长河中，选择那些最璀璨的明珠，通过讲故事的方式，介绍给学习汉语的外国学生和对中国文化感兴趣的外国读者。这些故事描述中国与其他国家、民族在各个领域文化交流中的重要人物、事件和现象，以使外国读者能够更深入地理解中国，理解中国文明，理解中国文明与其他各文明之间的密切关系，以及中国人和中国文明在这种交流过程中所作出的努力和贡献，并尽力彰显人类共同的精神追求与价值取向。

　　本书讲述的是中国元代剧作家纪君祥的《赵氏孤儿》西传欧洲、被法国文豪伏尔泰改编为《中国孤儿》的历史故事，这一部中国悲剧不断地被各国翻译、评论和改编，使欧洲在18世纪中期风行起了强大的"赵氏孤儿"热，也把欧洲在17世纪末兴起的"中国热"逐步推向了顶峰。

I

"The Orphan" Taken to Europe

In February 1734, an anonymous letter was carried by *Mercury*, an open publication in Paris. In this letter, snippets from the French translation of a Chinese drama were included. The letter said: "Sir, this is the new and unique present I promised to give you. Please tell me what you and your friends think after reading the Chinese tragedy. Furthermore, please also tell me the reason why I'm so interested in this drama. Is it because anything ancient or from far away can always stir our admiration?"

Who was the writer of this letter? How did he get to know this Chinese drama? Why was he so keen to introduce and recommend this "Chinese tragedy" to his French friends? Which "Chinese tragedy" was it referring to in this letter?

Although this letter was anonymous, people, through various channels, came to know that the writer of this letter was Joseph Henry Marie de Premar (1666–1736), a priest of the Society of Jesus in France.

1
"孤儿"被带到欧洲

1734年2月,在法国巴黎公开发行的《水星杂志》上,刊载了一篇没有署名的信。此信中有数处摘录了一部译成法文的中国戏剧的片断,信中说:"先生,这就是我答应给你的一件新鲜别致的东西。请你告诉我,你和你的朋友们看了这部中国悲剧觉得怎样。此外,还请你告诉我,我之所以对这部戏发生兴趣,是不是由于这样的一种心情,即凡是时代较古或地区较远的东西总能够引起我们的仰慕。"

这封信的作者是谁?他是从何得知这部中国的戏剧的?又为什么如此热切地要把这部"中国悲剧"推荐给他的法国朋友?信中所提到的究竟是哪一部"中国悲剧"?

虽然这封公开发表的信件没有署名,人们还是通过各种途径,得知这封信的作者就是法国耶稣会

Joseph Henrg Marie de Premar was born in Cherbourg in northwestern France on July 17, 1666. This was a town and seaport on the northern tip of Cotentin peninsula in Normandy. In 1683, he joined the Society of Jesus of the French diocese at the age of 18.

After joining the Christian Church, he was fully devoted to the study of theology and performed well. In 1698, he was sent to China as a missionary to disseminate Christianity. After his arrival in China, he was profoundly immersed in the Chinese culture and had never left China ever since, till his death in 1736. Furthermore, he also got a Chinese name—Ma Yuese.

Why did Ma Yuese write that letter? Why did he make

The European ship in the 13th century.

伏尔泰与《中国孤儿》

耶稣会士利玛窦和汤若望，他们正展开一幅中国地图。在他们的上方，是两位耶稣会的创始人。
Matteo Ricci and Johann Adam Schall von Bell opened a map of China. Above them there were two founders of Jesuits.

传教士约瑟夫·普雷马雷（1666—1736）。

1666年7月17日，约瑟夫·普雷马雷出生在法国西北部的瑟堡，这是诺曼底科唐坦半岛最北端的一个城镇和海港。在他18岁的时候，也就是1683年，他加入了法国教区的耶稣会。

加入耶稣会后，他一直非常努力地学习神学知识，表现非常优异。1698年，他被派往中国传播基督教。到中国后，他深深地被中国文化吸引，从此就再也没有离开过中国，直到1736年去世。此外，他还给自己起了个中国名字——马约瑟。

马约瑟为什么会写上面那封信呢？为什么又特别提到那部中国悲剧呢？以及耶稣会为什么要派他到中国进行传教呢？要想弄清这些问题，我们还需要先弄

11

a special mention of that Chinese tragedy? And why did the Society of Jesus send him to China as a missionary? In order to understand these questions, we should, first of all, know something about the age in which Ma Yuese lived.

In the late 17th century, some European merchants shipped some "made-in-China" commodities back to Europe, such as silk, porcelain, tea, lacquer and jade. When these commodities were available on the European market, they were sold out quickly. For the Europeans then, these made-in-China commodities were very exotic and attractive. They had never seen such fine and light silk products before, or imagined that the leaf-like stuff called "tea" could be drunk and could produce such a fresh scent and aroma. Neither had they seen a piece of furniture made of wood that could be so artistically made and so beautifully decorated.

Not only these "made-in-China" commodities were passionately pursued and cherished by the Europeans, the Chinese living habits were also imitated by some Europeans. In ancient China, sedan chair was a common and widely-used means of transport. In the eyes of Europeans, however, it was fun and interesting to use sedan chair as a means of transport. When French King Louis XIV was organizing a family party, he, after all guests had arrived, appeared at the party, sitting in a

楚马约瑟所处时代的一些状况。

17世纪末,一些欧洲的商人把丝绸、瓷器、茶叶、漆器、玉器等中国制造的物品贩运回欧洲,这些商品一投放到欧洲市场,就被疯狂抢购。这些"中国制造",对于当时的欧洲人,是那么的稀奇,那么的具有吸引力。他们从没有见过如此轻盈的丝织品;也从未想到如草叶般的叫做"茶"的东西竟然能泡着喝,并且散发出淡淡的清香;也没有见过木头制作的

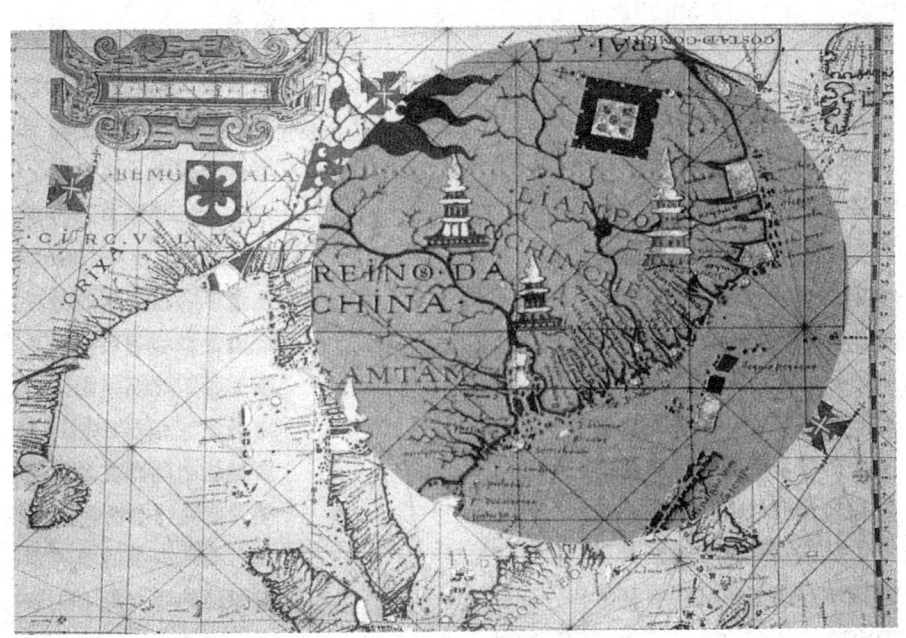

葡萄牙人1571年绘制的东方地图
A map of the East drawn by Portuguese in 1571.

Chinese sedan chair carried by eight servants. His guests were all surprised and shocked by his action.

Where China had so many fun and incredible "made-in-China" commodities, European merchants tried every means possible to ship them back to Europe to make money. Some aristocrats and nobles in Europe who were ready to be in the chic also wanted to own more "made-in-China" commodities. On the one hand, they could satisfy their curiosity, and on the other hand, they could show off.

Then, the Europeans found that the Chinese did not believe in God and Jesus Christ. How could Chinese not believe in God and Jesus Christ? The societies of Jesus in Europe perceived that it was necessary to bring the gospel from the God to the Chinese people and to convert them into children of the God.

Arranged by the European churches, some priests from the societies of Jesus came to China.

China had such a vast territory and a huge population, and priests sent to China were far from enough. So they asked the European churches to send more priests to China.

It was very costly to send missionaries to China to preach, and thus the churches had to consider the request prudentially. Furthermore, the Chinese people had their own traditional beliefs, and such beliefs seemed to have

家具，也可以如此装饰精美。

不仅是这些"中国制造"的商品受到欧洲人的热捧，而且中国人的生活习惯也成为一些欧洲人的模仿对象。在古代的中国，轿子是一种非常普通、常见的交通工具，而乘坐轿子在欧洲人眼里是那么的有趣。法国国王路易十四有一次举行家庭舞会时，等所有的客人都到齐后，他让八个人抬着一顶仿制的中国轿子出场了，所有客人都惊奇得目瞪口呆，感觉不可思议。

中国有着如此多的好玩的"中国制造"，欧洲商人总想尽可能把它们运回欧洲，赚上大把的钞票。欧洲一些追求时髦的达官贵族，他们也想得到更多的"中国制造"，一方面满足自己的好奇心，一方面向人展示自己的时尚。

同时，欧洲人也发现，中国不信仰上帝和基督。不

1625至1650年间的中国青花瓷罐，上有基督教图案，反映了基督教在中国的存在和影响。
Chinese porcelain jar with Christian design between 1625 and 1650, denoting the existence and influence of Christianity in China.

17世纪西方人描绘的中国沿海城市福州
The Panorama of Fuzhou, a coastal city of southeastern China, painted by a westerner in the 17th century.

been deeply rooted in their mind and heart, and there were few Chinese people willing to accept the dogma preached by the missionaries. Therefore, the European missionaries failed to achieve their desirable effect in their preaching in China, and this was also the reason that the European churches were reluctant to send more priests and missionaries to China.

The missionaries in China were deeply impressed by the profoundness of Chinese culture, and also perceived a good

信仰上帝与基督怎么行呢？于是，欧洲的基督教会感觉到有必要把上帝的福音带给中国人，让他们也成为上帝的好孩子。

在欧洲教会的安排下，一些耶稣会的传教士来到了中国。

中国的土地实在是太广，人口也实在是多，来中国传教的传教士发现人手远远不够用。于是，他们就

1275年，元世祖忽必烈在上都夏宫（今内蒙古多伦北）接见了来自意大利的波罗一家，包括父亲尼科洛·波罗、叔父马泰奥·波罗和年幼的马可·波罗。
Kublai Khan received Nicolo Polo, Maffeo Polo and Marco Polo in 1275.

prospect for their preaching in China. So, they tried hard to persuade the churches to accept their suggestions to send more priests and missionaries to China and to strengthen the preaching services in China. At that time, any direct request seemed not working. Then, the missionaries began to introduce more information about China to Europe so that the European churches could have a deeper understanding about China. When they got a deeper understanding about China, it would be probable that they would send more priests and missionaries to China.

向欧洲总教会请求，希望总教会能够多派些传教士到中国。

派传教士到中国进行传教，是要花费很多经费的。对此，总教会不能不慎重考虑。而且，中国人有着自己的传统信仰，而且这些信仰似乎是扎根于他们的头脑中的，很少有中国人愿意接受传教士的教义。因而，欧洲传教士在中国的传教效果不是很明显，这也让欧洲总教会在向中国增派更多传教士的问题上，颇有顾虑。

在中国的传教士都深切感受到中国文化的博大精

葡萄牙人所描绘的中国人形象
Portraits of Chinese, drawn by Portuguese.

17世纪西方绘画作品，描绘了最早进入东方的耶稣会士沙勿略在传教过程中遭遇的艰辛和苦难。
A western painting in the 17th century, described the hardships faced by S. Franciscus Xaverius during missionizing in the East.

The missionaries in China wrote beautiful stories and articles about what they saw in China and sent them back to Europe. There were numerous copies of such stories and articles, and the articles covered virtually every aspect of China.

Take Alvaro Semedo (1585–1658) from the Portugal Society of Jesus for example. He came to China to preach in 1613. In 1616, he was expelled from China because he did not obey the Chinese government rules and made too

深，也感觉中国的传教前景应该是比较好的。于是，他们就想说服总教会接受他们的建议，增派更多的传教士到中国，来加强在中国的传教事业。当时，直白的请求是行不通的，于是，他们就想把中国的一些信息介绍到欧洲，让欧洲总教会对中国有一些更深入的了解，这样，也许就会有可能增派更多的传教士到中国来了。

在中国的传教士把他们在中国的所见所闻，写成了一篇篇优美的文章，寄回欧洲。这样的文章是非常

16世纪末欧洲人眼中的中国人
The images of Chinese in westerner's eyes in the end of 16th century.

much trouble. He, however, loved China very much and also loved to conduct the preaching services in China. In 1620, he could no longer hold back his desire for China and came to preach in China again. This time, however, he learned his lesson, no longer tried to make trouble and was fully devoted to the preaching service. He also knew clearly that the number of missionaries to China was too small and it was detrimental to the development of the preaching services. Moreover, he wanted Europe to send more priests and missionaries to China to work

1729年出版的《耶稣会士中国书简集》中收录的康熙皇帝画像
A portrait of Emperor Kangxi, embodied in *Letters of the Missionary Jesuits*.

together with him and to conduct the preaching services in China. Based on what he saw and experienced in China, he wrote a book entitled *The History of the Chinese Empire*. In this book, he made detailed and vivid descriptions about China, including the history of the name of China, its geographical location, territory, land, products, arts and crafts, science and technology, government institutions, social system, the language, prisons and workmanship.

Take Martino Martini (1614–1661) from the Italian

伏尔泰与《中国孤儿》

多的，对中国的介绍，也几乎包括了中国的方方面面。

如葡萄牙耶稣会士曾德昭（1585—1658），他于1613年到中国传教。1616年，他因不听从中国政府的管理，寻衅闹事，被赶出了中国。不过，他早已真正喜欢上了中国，也喜欢在中国进行的传教事业。到1620年，他实在难以抑制再次到中国传教的欲望，于是就返回中国。不过这次他学乖了，不再胡闹滋事了，而是一心进行传教工作。他也深感在中国的传教士人少，对于传教事业的发展不利，也想让欧洲总教会能派更多的传教士到达中国，好与他并肩作战，做好在中国的传教事业。他根据在中国的一切见闻，写出了一部《中华帝国史》。在此书中，他对中国作了非常详细而生动的介绍，包括中国名称的来历、地理位置、疆域、土地、物产、工艺、科技、政府机构、社会制度、汉语言、监狱、技艺等各个方面。

曾德昭像
A portrait of Alvare Semedo.

23

Society of Jesus for another example. He came to China to preach in 1643. In about 10 years of his preaching services in China, he traveled across nine provinces, almost half of the Chinese territory. When he arrived in China, it was the time of a major historical change in the Chinese history—the downfall of the Ming Dynasty (1368–1644) and the rise and establishment of the Qing Dynasty (1616–1911). He had the opportunity to witness the entire process of the historical change, and wrote about this significant event in his book entitled *De Bello Tartarico Historia*, describing in details the true process of the change from the Ming Dynasty to the Qing Dynasty, and reporting back to Europe what was happening then in China. He pointed out in this book that the fall of the Ming Dynasty was the consequence of the maladies with the Ming Dynasty government and was the result from the fact that the public no longer had confidence in it. Although the Manchus were fairly barbarian and ignorant before the fall of the Ming Dynasty, they, after seizing Beijing, made great efforts in learning the cultural traditions of central China and in improving their cultural attainment. The Ming Dynasty was overthrown and was no longer in existence, but the Chinese traditional civilization continued without interruption, and this showed the advantages of the traditional Chinese culture. Martino Martini not only wrote this book on the latest

再如意大利耶稣会士卫匡国（1614—1661），他是在1643年到中国传教的。他在中国传教有大约有十年的时间，走遍了南北九省，几乎是半个中国。他刚到中国时，正好遇到了明朝（1368—1644）灭亡、清朝（1616—1911）建立的中国历史上的重大变革，他目睹了整个事件的发展过程，于是他就把这颇具新闻性的事件写成了《鞑靼战纪》一书，描述了明、清朝代更替的真实过程，向欧洲通报中国正在发生的事情。他还在这部书中指出：明朝灭亡是由于明朝政府自身存在着很多的弊病，是老百姓对它失去信任而导致的结果；满人虽然在灭亡明朝以前比较野蛮、蒙昧，但在攻占北京后，就努力学习中原的文化传统，提高自身的文化素养。虽然明朝灭亡了，但中国传统的文明却没有中断，这充分显出中国传统文化的优越性。卫匡国不仅写

卫匡国《中国上古史》封面
The cover of *Ancient History of China* by Martino Martini.

happenings in China, but also wrote books such as *New History of China* and *Ancient History of China* to introduce China's geography, arts, customs, urban construction and historical development to Europe.

There were many more books on China written by Jesuits, and their goal was to persuade the European churches to send more priests and missionaries to China. Under such circumstances, Ma Yuese, who studied hard and performed well, was sent by the Society of Jesus to preach in Jiangxi Province of China.

In Jiangxi, Ma Yuese did not take preaching as his prime task. Instead, he arranged his assistants to do the preaching services, and he himself was devoted to learning the Chinese language. Shortly afterwards, he basically knew how to read and write the Chinese characters. Then, he began to extensively read the Chinese books. To him, the Chinese people were so devout to their traditions, then should the Chinese books contain anything similar to the Christian dogma? If there were similarities and common grounds, it would be preferable to make use of them to promote the preaching services so as to enhance the preaching effects.

His practice, however, did not win understanding from other missionaries in China, and the European churches did not ratify his practice either. Ma Yuese, however, insisted on what he was doing, and continued to make

了这部反映中国最新事件的书,他还著有《中国新图志》和《中国上古史》,向欧洲介绍中国的地理、人文、风俗、城市建设和历史发展等多个方面的情况。

由耶稣会士撰写的其他介绍中国的著作还有很多,目的都是想说服欧洲总教会增派更多的传教士到中国来。正是在这种情形下,学习刻苦、成绩优异的马约瑟,被耶稣会派到中国江西传教。

在江西,马约瑟并没有把传教作为首要任务,而是把具体的传教任务交给了助手,他本人则是日夜学习汉语。很快,他就基本掌握了汉字的识读与书写。于是,他就开始大量阅读中国书籍。他想,既然中国人如此敬仰自己的传统,那么,在中国书籍中,是否有着与基督教教义相通的地方呢?如果有相通的地方,也许就可以借助这些相通的地方,来进行传教工作,就可以增强传教的效果。

但是,他的这一做法,却没有得到同在中国传教的其他传教士的理解,欧洲的总教会对他的这一做法也不认可。可是,马约瑟仍然坚持自己的这一做法,不断地把自己的研究成果写成文字,寄回欧洲。对于马约瑟的一意孤行,欧洲总教会非常生气,要求在欧

written records of his research findings and sent them back to Europe. When Ma Yuese continued to go his own way, the European churches got very angry with him, and requested some publications in Europe not to publish the articles by Ma Yuese. They wanted to force Ma Yuese to toe the line of the churches by the way of blocking the publishing of his articles.

However, Ma Yuese was very stubborn and did not want to give up his idea. He wanted very much to make his research findings public and to let the public understand and accept his practice. He also believed that there was only one way that he could get his articles published, that was, he did not sign his name to the articles. Due to this reason, as mentioned at the beginning of this chapter, we read that anonymous letter in *Mercury* magazine.

Ma Yuese translated a Chinese tragedy into French and sent it to his friends to read and enjoy. Ma Yuese named it *The Orphan of Zhao, a Chinese Tragedy*. From the title given by Ma Yuese, we could figure out that the drama in China should be *The Orphan of Zhao*.

For a long time, the European churches did not allow articles by Ma Yuese to be published. By 1734, Ma Yuese had become aged and his physical conditions were getting ever poorer, and he knew that his old age was coming. He, however, continued to stick to his belief and did not

伏尔泰与《中国孤儿》

广彩人物碟,这是为法国商人所订造的,碟上法文图案的意思是"忠诚和坚贞"。
Guangcai dish painted with figures and inscribed with French motto.

洲的一些刊物杜绝刊载马约瑟的文章,想通过这种方法来封杀马约瑟,逼迫他向总教会就范。

但马约瑟非常倔强,他不想放弃自己的想法。他一心想把自己的成果公布于众,让世人了解自己的做法。他认为只有一个办法可以发表自己的文章,那就是文章不署他自己的名字。正是因为这样,所以如开篇所述,我们在《水星杂志》上所看到的那封信,是没有署名的。

change. In the year, Ma Yuese heard that two missionaries, Weller and Brossel, were to return to France from China. He met them and asked them to take the translation version of *The Orphan of the Zhao, a Chinese Tragedy* back to France and to deliver it to Etienne Fourmont (1683–1745), an influential personage in France. He hoped that Fourmont could help him to have his articles published in Europe.

But something went wrong in the process. Weller and Brossel did not hand over *The Orphan of the Zhao, a Chinese Tragedy* to Fourmont, but instead, sent it to Father Jean-Baptiste Du Halde (1674–1743).

Father Du Halde was the secretary to the master who presided over the confessions by French King Louis XIV, and was responsible for organizing the work of Jesuits in China. From 1709, he acted as the chief editor of *Letters of the Missionary Jesuits*. This was an annual publication of letters sponsored by the Society of Jesus, and it mainly published the written reports submitted to Jesuits from abroad to the societies of Jesus. At the same time, in order to avoid political troubles and attacks from some other churches, necessary selection was made when the letters were chosen for publication. With this selection process, some materials would not be able to get published. Feeling pitiful for those reports and materials abandoned, Father Du Halde got the idea to turn these "wastes" into

马约瑟把一部中国悲剧翻译成了法文，要交给他的朋友欣赏。马约瑟还给它起了个名字，叫做《中国悲剧〈赵氏孤儿〉》。从马约瑟所起的这个名字我们可以看出，在中国，这部传统悲剧的名字应该是《赵氏孤儿》。

很长一段时间，欧洲总教会不允许马约瑟的文章在欧洲公开发表。到了1734年，马约瑟年纪已经比较大了，身体状况也不是太好，他深感暮年即将来临。但是，他那颗坚持己见的心，并没有改变。这一年，马约瑟听说维莱尔和布罗塞两位在中国的传教士要回法国，于是就找到他们，请求他们把翻译好的《中国悲剧〈赵氏孤儿〉》带回法国，交给在法国比较有影响的人物傅尔蒙（1683—1745）。他希望傅尔蒙帮助他，让他的文章能够在欧洲公开发表。

不知道捎带过程中出现了什么问题，维莱尔与布罗塞两位传教士并没有把《中国悲剧〈赵氏孤儿〉》转交给傅尔蒙，而是送到了杜赫德神父（1674—1743）手里。

杜赫德神父是法国国王路易十四的忏悔师的秘书，并负责统筹在中国的耶稣会士的工作。从1709年

treasures. So, he compiled the abandoned reports and published them in another book. When these "wastes" were compiled, the book, *Description of the Empire of China and Chinese-Tartary, Together with the Kingdoms of Korea and Tibet; Containing the Geography and History (Natural as well as Civil) of Those Countries*, was published in 1735. This book contained the articles by 27 Jesuits describing China's geography, history, politics, religions, economy, folk customs, specialties, education, language, literature and philosophy. The *Orphan of Zhao, a Chinese Tragedy* translated by Ma Yuese was one of the articles by the 27 Jesuits.

When *The Orphan of Zhao, a Chinese Tragedy* translated by Ma Yuese was given to Father Du Halde, he was compiling the *Description of the Empire of China and Chinese-Tartary, Together with the Kingdoms of Korea and Tibet; Containing the Geography and History (Natural as well as Civil) of Those Countries*. He was so delighted that, without obtaining consent from the translator, he included the translation, without any hesitation, into his book and had it published.

The Orphan of Zhao, a Chinese Tragedy was so mistakenly sent to Father Du Halde, and got published in France. Immediately after the book made its debut, it caused a stir in the literary circles and received warm recognition. Some commented and spoke highly of it, some created

开始，他任《耶稣会士书简集》主编。这是由耶稣会主办的一年一期的书信集，主要是发表国外耶稣会士向耶稣总会提交的书面报告。同时，为了避免一些政治上的麻烦和其他一些教会的攻击，在编选报告集出版时，就不得不进行必要的选择。经过选择，就会造成一些材料无法采用出版。对于这些被舍弃的材料，杜赫德神父感觉非常惋惜，于是就产生了把这些"废弃物"变废为宝的想法。这样，杜赫德神父就把这些舍弃的书面报告，另外编辑成书出版，与读者见面。把这些"废弃物"结集后，就有了1735年出版的《中华帝国全志》一书。此书内容包括了中国地理、历史、政治、宗教、经济、民俗、特产、教育、语言、文学、哲学等各方面的情况，共由27人的作品组成。在这27人的作品中，就有马约瑟翻译的《中国悲剧〈赵氏孤儿〉》。

当马约瑟翻译的《中国悲剧〈赵氏孤儿〉》交到杜赫德神父手里时，他正在编辑《中华帝国全志》一书，他喜出望外，在没有征得翻译者同意的情况下，就毫不犹豫地把它收进了《中华帝国全志》，并随即公开发行。

their own versions through imitation, some translated the French version into other languages, and some translated it again from original Chinese version of *The Orphan of Zhao*. Of them, the drama, *The Orphan of China*, adapted and re-created from *The Orphan of Zhao* by Voltaire (1694–1778), was particularly noteworthy. Due to the prestigious position and influence of Voltaire in the French literary circles and the huge success of the premiere of his work *The Orphan of China*, the "China fever" already spreading across Europe was further promoted.

In this unexpected way, *The Orphan of Zhao* was taken to Europe.

就这样,这部《中国悲剧〈赵氏孤儿〉》阴差阳错地被送到杜赫德神父手里后,得以在法国公开出版发行。《中国悲剧〈赵氏孤儿〉》与读者一见面,立即引起了文学界的强烈关注,有的对其品头论足,有的进行模仿创作,有的是把法文翻译成其他文字再版,有的则是把中国原版的《赵氏孤儿》再次翻译。在这当中,尤为值得称道的,是伏尔泰(1694—1778)由《赵氏孤儿》改编创作的《中国孤儿》一剧。由于伏尔泰本人在法国文学界的地位及影响,以及他创作的《中国孤儿》在巴黎上演的巨大成功,进一步推动了当时弥漫于欧洲的"中国热"。

就这样,《赵氏孤儿》被带到了欧洲。

Society of Jesus

Society of Jesus was one of the major Catholic orders and Congregations, and it was also called the Jesuits. It was founded on August 15, 1535, by Ignace de Loyola from Spain in line with the religious reforms of the Protestantism and won the approval from the Church of Rome. The main tasks of the Society of Jesus were education and preaching. They established many universities in Europe and helped to train, in addition to Jesuits, persons in the political and the intellectual circles, and the most famous of them was René Descartes, famous philosopher, mathematician and physicist in France.

Fourmont

Fourmont was a renowned sinologist in France and also the first sinologist of France. In 1711, Arcade Huang (1679–1716, once served as a Chinese language translator for the royal family of French King Louis XIV), a Chinese who studied in France, needed to find an assistant, and Fourmont was recommended to him. Fourmont was previously a professor of Arabic and did not know Chinese. After he became an assistant for Arcade Huang, he shifted to learn the Chinese language and the China studies. From then on, he was fully devoted to sinology and became the most influential sinologist in France. Due to his influence in the sinology circles in France, Ma Yuese asked him to look over and examine his research findings related to China, and hoped that Fourmont could help him have his research findings and articles published in France.

耶稣会

耶稣会为天主教的主要修会之一,又称耶稣连队,1535年8月15日由西班牙罗耀拉的依纳爵因应当时基督新教的宗教改革成立,获得罗马教廷教宗的许可。耶稣会最主要的任务是教育与传教,在欧洲兴办许多大学,培养出的学生除了是耶稣会人才外,也活跃于政界与知识分子阶层,著名的如法国哲学家、数学家、物理学家笛卡儿。

傅尔蒙

傅尔蒙是法国著名的汉学专家,也是法国第一位汉学专家。在1711年,留法的中国人黄嘉略(1679—1716,曾任法国国王路易十四的皇家汉语翻译员)需要一位助手,就有人把傅尔蒙介绍给了他。傅尔蒙原来是阿拉伯文教授,并不懂汉语。他跟随黄嘉略后,就转而致力于汉语的学习和对中国的研究,从此与汉学结下不解之缘,并成为法国具有重要影响的汉学家。正是由于他在法国汉学界的这种影响,马约瑟才将自己的有关中国的研究成果请他过目,并希望他能帮助自己在法国刊发。

II

The Story of "The Orphan of Zhao"

To get to know the story of *The Orphan of Zhao*, we must start with *Records of the Historian* by Sima Qian (45–after 87 BC) of the Han Dynasty (206 BC–220 AD).

For generations, Sima Qian's family were royal historiographers, officials who specialized in compiling books of events that actually took place for rulers. Sima Qian's father, Sima Tan, was determined to compile a historical book recording the historical events of past dynasties, but was unable to realize this goal before his death, so he asked Sima Qian to fulfill his long-cherished wish in front of the sickbed. After his father died, 38-year-old Sima Qian inherited his father's position and unfulfilled wish, extensively read various literatures and materials, carried out folk investigations, and collected folk tales and legends to make preparations for compiling a general history. He started to write *Records of the Historian* at the age of 42.

2

"赵氏孤儿"的故事

司马迁像
A portrait of Sima Qian.

要了解《赵氏孤儿》的故事，我们必须要从汉代（前206—公元220）司马迁（前145—前87年后）的《史记》说起。

司马迁的家族世代为皇家史官，就是专门为统治者把现实中发生的事件编撰成书的官员。司马迁的父亲司马谈，曾立志要编撰一部记载历代历史事件的史书，但直到去世前他仍没有实现这一愿望，于是他临终前就在病榻上嘱托司马迁一定要完成其夙愿。父亲去世后，38岁的司马迁继承了父亲的职位和遗志，广泛阅读各种文献资料，并进行民间调查，搜集民间的传说轶闻，为编撰一部通史作准备，于42岁时开始写

Later, because of his defense of General Li Ling who surrendered to the Huns, Sima Qian, without enough money to redeem himself, was sentenced to castration by Emperor Wu of the Han Dynasty (156–87 BC). This was nothing else than a crying shame for a man, but Sima Qian fulfilled his father's last wish, turned the shame into a strong motivation, and plunged into compiling the *Records of the Historian* that "studies the limits of heaven and man, records the changes of all times and forms an original system of thought." It is China's first general history presented in a series of biographies, recording China's political, economic and cultural development during more than 3,000 years from the times of the legendary Yellow Emperor to the reign of Emperor Wu of the Western Han Dynasty and consisting of five parts: Imperial Biographies (recording the deeds of emperors), Biographies of the Feudal Houses and Eminent Persons (recording the deeds of princes, marquises and relatives of kings and emperors), Biographies and Collective Biographies (recording people whose deeds could be described in the author's opinion), Tables (chronology of events) and Treatises (recording laws and regulations of past dynasties). It exerted a profound influence on later ages.

The contents of *Records of the Historian* are so profound and extensive that almost all historical events during and

《史记》书影
Records of the Historian.

作《史记》。

后来，由于为当时一个投降匈奴的汉将李陵辩护，司马迁无钱自赎，被汉武帝（前156—前87）处以宫刑。这对于男人来说无异于奇耻大辱，但司马迁为了完成父亲的遗愿，化耻辱为动力，全身心地编撰了"究天人之际，通古今之变，成一家之言"的《史记》。这是中国第一部纪传体通史，记载了上自传说中的黄帝下至西汉汉武帝约三千余年的中国政治、经济、文化各方面的发展，分为本纪（记载帝王的事迹）、世家（记载王侯外戚事迹）、列传（记载作者认为行迹可状之人）、表（大事年表）和书（记载历代典章制度）五个部分，对后世影响深远。

before the reign of Emperor Wu can be found in it. An account of the story of "The Orphan of Zhao" can also be found in this book.

The chapter of *Records of the Historian—The House of Zhao* specially records the rise and decline of the Zhao family. When Prince Chong'er of the Jin State was in distress, Zhao Shuai, the great grandfather of the orphan of Zhao, went through thick and thin with Chong'er and helped him to become the king of Jin State, i.e. Duke Wen of Jin. Therefore, he was put into an important position by Chong'er and became a powerful figure in Jin State.

晋文公重耳像
A portrait of Duke Wen of Jin, Chong'er.

After Zhao Shuai's death, his son Zhao Dun inherited his position and enjoyed all powers possessed by Zhao Shuai. In the 8th year of the reign of Duke Xiang of Jin, Duke Xiang died. At that time, crown prince Yigao was still young and the situation of Jin State's neighborhood was unfavorable. So Zhao Dun wanted to avoid the crown prince and let the younger brother of Duke Xiang of Jin in Qin State inherit the crown. But by convention, if the king died and there was a crown prince, the crown

赵盾像
A portrait of Zhao Dun.

　　《史记》内容涵盖深广，武帝及武帝前的历史事件几乎都能在其中找到相应的记载，我们所要了解的"赵氏孤儿"的故事，也能在此书中找到相应的表述。

　　《史记·赵世家》一章，是专门记载赵氏一族的兴衰过程的。赵氏孤儿的曾祖父名叫赵衰，他在晋国公子重耳落难时，与重耳患难与共，并帮助重耳做了晋国国王，即晋文公。由此他受到了晋文公重耳的重用，在晋国位高权重。

　　赵衰去世后，他的儿子赵盾继承了他的职位，享有赵衰所拥有的一切权力。在晋襄公八年，襄公逝世。这时太子夷皋年纪还小，而且晋国所面临的周边局势又不利，赵盾就想避开太子，迎接还在秦国的晋襄公的弟弟来继承王位。但是按照惯例，如果国王去世，有太子在，一定要立太子为新的国王，无论太子多么年幼。若是另立别人为新的继承人，无异于宣判

prince, however young, must be installed as the new king. Installing another person as the new inheritor was nothing else than sentencing the crown prince to death. Of course, crown prince Yigao was ignorant of the advantages and disadvantages of Zhao Dun's decision, but the crown prince's mother knew them clearly and could not accept this reality. So the crown prince's mother cried day and night and complained tearfully to Zhao Dun. Zhao Dun also thought that although the crown prince was young, he had done nothing wrong and that should he insist on letting the younger brother of Duke Xiang of Jin inherit the crown and depose the crown prince with no reason, he might cause an unnecessary disaster, so he had to let crown prince Yigao inherit the crown. Thus crown prince Yigao became Duke Ling of Jin.

In more than ten years of his reign, Duke Ling of Jin was extravagant, dissipated and extremely atrocious. He killed a cook who did not fully cook bear paws, and Zhao Dun happened to hear about it. Zhao Dun was usually very strict with Duke Ling of Jin and hoped that he would become a wise king and make Jin State stronger.

Duke Ling of Jin was afraid that Zhao Dun would admonish him again because he killed the cook for no reason, so he sent a person to assassinate Zhao Dun. However, Zhao Dun was usually very kindhearted to ordinary people, and all of them loved and respected him.

了太子死刑。对于赵盾的这种决定，太子夷皋当然还不明白其中的利害。但太子的母亲非常清楚，也无法接受。于是，太子的母亲就日夜啼哭，并向赵盾哭诉。赵盾也想，太子虽然年幼，但也没有什么过错，如果自己执意让晋襄公的弟弟继承王位，没有任何理由地废除太子，也许会招致不必要的祸害，就只好让太子夷皋继位。这样，太子夷皋就成为了晋灵公。

晋灵公继位十余年，骄奢淫逸、残暴无度，曾因厨师没有把熊掌做到十成熟而把厨师给杀了。这件事恰巧又让赵盾知道了。平时赵盾对晋灵公要求又比较严格，希望他能成为一代明君，把晋国治理得更加强大。

晋灵公怕因他无端杀害厨师，赵盾又要劝谏他，就派人去暗杀赵盾。不过赵盾平日是对百姓仁爱有加，百姓都非常爱戴、尊敬他。晋灵公指派的这个杀手就曾经受过赵盾的恩惠，于是就放走了赵盾。

赵盾逃到边境时，他的兄弟赵穿把晋灵公给杀了，并让晋襄公的弟弟做了国王。于是赵盾就没有逃出边境，继续回到首都做他的大臣。晋襄公的弟弟就成了晋成公。赵盾的这一做法，引起了很多人的不满，认为赵盾这样做不合为臣之道，应该为晋灵公报

The assassin sent by Duke Ling of Jin was once favored by Zhao Dun, so he let Zhao Dun go.

When Zhao Dun escaped to the border, his brother Zhao Chuan killed Duke Ling of Jin and let the younger brother of Duke Xiang of Jin become the king, so Zhao Dun did not escape across the border. He went back to the capital and continued to serve as a minister. The younger brother of Duke Xiang of Jin became Duke Cheng of Jin. This act of Zhao Dun made many people discontent. They thought that this act of Zhao Dun violated the principle of being a subject and that Zhao Dun should kill Zhao Chuan, take the blame and resign to avenge Duke Ling of Jin. But Zhao Dun really applied a policy of benevolence and won the trust of Duke Cheng of Jin. He held power in his hands and was not affected.

One day, Zhao Dun had a dream. A dream interpreter said that this dream implied: Because of Zhao Dun's "regicide," his descendants would suffer disasters.

Zhao Dun died when Duke Jing of Jin was the king, and his son Zhao Shuo inherited his position. Zhao Shuo's wife was the younger sister of Duke Cheng of Jin. At that time, Tu Angu, another minister, was put into an important position by Duke Jing of Jin. In the 3rd year of the reign of Duke Jing of Jin, Tu Angu wanted to kill the entire Zhao family to avenge the personal wrongs. So he again brought up the fact that Zhao Chuan killed

仇，杀死赵穿，自己引咎辞职。不过赵盾确实行使仁政，且受到晋成公的信任，大权在手，也就没有受到什么影响。

有一天，赵盾做了一个梦，经人解梦，说这个梦暗示：由于赵盾"弑君"这件事，他的后人将要遭受灾难。

晋景公当国时，赵盾去世，他的儿子赵朔继承他的职位，而赵朔的妻子是晋成公的妹妹。当时晋景公重用另一大臣屠岸贾，在晋景公三年，屠岸贾为报私仇想杀了赵氏全家。于是他就重提当年赵穿杀害晋灵公而赵盾不为晋灵公报仇的事，并在朝中大肆宣扬，说赵盾就是杀害晋灵公的幕后主使，赵盾的子孙不能在朝为官，并且要受到惩罚。

将军韩厥劝说屠岸贾不要这么做，并称赵盾是无罪的。韩厥曾提前通知赵朔屠岸贾要杀害他的消息，让赵朔赶快逃跑。但是赵朔没有逃跑，而是向韩厥提出：如果他不想让赵家断子绝孙，就不要帮屠岸贾一起杀害赵氏家族。韩厥答应了赵朔的要求，终不肯参与残害赵家。屠岸贾一意孤行，并假传晋景公的命令，瞒着韩厥，就和其他官员一起攻进赵盾儿子赵朔

Duke Ling of Jin and Zhao Dun did not avenge Duke Ling of Jin, and made lots of publicity efforts in the court, claiming that Zhao Dun was the mastermind of the killing of Duke Ling of Jin and that Zhao Dun's descendants should not become officials in the court and should be punished.

General Han Jue tried to persuade Tu Angu not to do this and said Zhao Dun was innocent. Han Jue informed Zhao Shuo beforehand that Tu Angu wanted to kill him and asked Zhao Shuo to escape quickly, but Zhao Shuo did not escape and proposed to Han Jue: If he did not want the Zhao family to have no descendants, he should not help Tu Angu kill the Zhao family. Han Jue accepted Zhao Shuo's request and ultimately refused to participate in the killing of the Zhao family. Tu Angu went his own way and gave a false order of Duke Jing of Jin. Keeping Han Jue in the dark, Tu Angu, together with other officials, charged into the residence of Zhao Shuo, Zhao Dun's son, and killed the Zhao family and family servants.

When Tu Angu massacred Zhao Shuo and his family, Zhao Shuo's wife was pregnant. Because she was a princess, she hurried to the home of Duke Cheng of Jin to hide and escaped death. Before long, Zhao Shuo's wife gave birth to a boy.

When Tu Angu heard about it, he sent men to search for the baby at the hiding-place of Zhao Shuo's wife, who

的住处，杀害了赵氏族人和家丁。

在屠岸贾残杀赵朔及其族人时，赵朔的妻子有孕在身，因身为公主就急忙躲到了晋成公的家里，得以幸免于难。不久，赵朔的妻子就产下了一个男婴。

屠岸贾听说后，就派人赶到赵朔妻子藏身的地方搜查婴儿。赵朔的妻子吓坏了，她为了保存赵家的血脉，情急之下，就把婴儿藏在了套裤内，并祷告说："如果上天要赵家断绝香火，士兵来搜查时，这个婴儿就会哭；如果上天不要赵家断绝香火，士兵来搜查时，这个婴儿就不会哭。"结果，屠岸贾派来的士兵搜查到赵朔妻子藏身处时，套裤内的婴儿竟然没有发出一点儿声响。这样，这个婴儿躲过了一劫。这个婴儿也就是赵氏孤儿。

赵朔的门客公孙杵臼和赵朔的朋友程婴商量，认为屠岸贾搜查不到赵氏孤儿，是不会善罢甘休的，要想个办法保全赵氏孤儿的性命。公孙杵臼问程婴："养育赵氏孤儿与选择死亡，哪件更难？"程婴回答道："选择死亡容易，养育赵氏孤儿艰难。"公孙杵臼说："赵家原来待你非常好，你应该来做艰难的事，而我应该做相对容易的事，我就先死吧。"然

was terrified. In order to preserve the lineage of the Zhao family, she hid the baby in leggings in an emergency and prayed: "If the God wants the Zhao family to have no descendants, this baby will cry when soldiers come to search; if God does not want the Zhao family to have no descendants, this baby will not cry when soldiers come to search." When the soldiers sent by Tu Angu searched the hiding-place of Zhao Shuo's wife, the baby in the leggings unexpectedly made no sound and thus escaped the disaster. This baby was the orphan of Zhao.

After a discussion, Zhao Shuo's hanger-on Gongsun Chujiu and Zhao Shuo's friend Cheng Ying thought that Tu Angu would not take it lying down if he failed to find the orphan of Zhao, and they must find a way to save the baby's life. Gongsun Chujiu said to Cheng Ying: "Is raising the orphan of Zhao more difficult or less difficult than choosing death?" Cheng Ying answered: "Choosing death is easy and raising the orphan of Zhao is difficult." Gongsun Chujiu said: "The Zhao family treated you well, so you should do the difficult thing and I should do the relatively easy thing. I'll die first." Then, the two of them made a plan and decided to find a baby about the same age and disguise him as the orphan of Zhao. They wrapped this fake orphan of Zhao in embroidered swaddling clothes and hid him in Gongsun Chujiu's home.

后，两人商量一计，决定找个与赵氏孤儿大小相当的孩子，来顶替赵氏孤儿。他们把这个假的赵氏孤儿用绣花的襁褓包好，藏到公孙杵臼家里。

程婴告诉屠岸贾派来搜寻赵氏孤儿的将军说："我程婴不肖，不能保存赵氏孤儿，谁能给我一千两黄金，我就告诉谁赵氏孤儿的藏匿地方。"听到程婴如此说，多位将军都答应程婴的条件。于是程婴就领着这些将军去找公孙杵臼。公孙杵臼就对着程婴大骂他见利忘义、出卖朋友，并抱着假的赵氏孤儿向搜查的将军说道："天呀！天呀！赵氏孤儿有什么罪？请让赵氏孤儿活下去吧，只杀了我公孙杵臼就行了。"众将军不答应，杀死了公孙杵臼和他怀抱着的婴儿。屠岸贾等人认为赵氏孤儿已经被杀死了。而真的赵氏孤儿和程婴就藏匿在深山中，程婴含辛茹苦把他抚养成人。

等赵氏孤儿15岁时，有一天晋景公生病，就占卜了一卦。卦象显示有在晋国功业不遂的人在作祟，致使晋景公生病。晋景公就问韩厥是谁受了冤屈，至今阴魂不散，前来索报。韩厥知道赵氏孤儿还活着，就说是赵氏宗族的鬼魂在作祟，因为赵氏一直帮助晋国国君治理国

Cheng Ying told the generals sent by Tu Angu to search for the orphan of Zhao: "I am unworthy and cannot keep the orphan of Zhao. Whoever gives me one thousand taels of silver, I will tell him the hiding-place of the orphan of Zhao." After hearing Cheng Ying's words, several generals consented to Cheng Ying's conditions. So Cheng Ying led these generals to look for Gongsun Chujiu. Gongsun Chujiu accused Cheng Ying of forgetting what was right at the sight of profit and betraying friends in front of him. Holding the fake orphan of Zhao in his arms, he said to the generals who came to search: "God! God! What crime did the orphan of Zhao commit? Please let the orphan of Zhao live and just kill me." The generals did not agree and killed Gongsun Chujiu and the baby he held in his arms. Tu Angu and others thought that the orphan of Zhao had been killed, while the real orphan of Zhao and Cheng Ying hid in remote mountains. Cheng Ying endured all kinds of hardships to bring him up.

When the orphan of Zhao was 15 years old, Duke Jing of Jin fell ill one day and so he divined by the Eight Diagrams. The result showed that a person who did not achieve success in Jin State was causing trouble, which led to his disease. Duke Jing of Jin asked Han Jue who was wronged and was still lingering on and seeking retribution. Han Jue knew that the orphan of Zhao was still alive. So he said the ghosts of the Zhao family had

家，功劳甚大，反受灭门之灾，全国的人民都为他们的遭遇感到不平。现在占卜显现此事，希望君主能够为这事做主，为赵氏宗族平反。晋景公就问："那赵氏宗族还有后代活在世上吗？"韩厥就把赵氏孤儿还活在世上的事告诉了晋景公。晋景公与韩厥商量要恢复赵氏宗族的名声，并在朝重用赵氏孤儿。

于是，他们秘密地把赵氏孤儿带到宫中。趁各位将领进宫探望晋景公时，韩厥让各位将领拜见赵氏孤儿。赵氏孤儿取名为赵武。诸位将领迫于形势，纷纷说道，"当时对赵氏家族发起屠杀，是因为屠岸贾假传国君的命令。如果不是这样，我们怎么敢对赵家发难呢？今天国君您要重用赵家后人，正是我们的心愿，我们惟命是从。"

这样，赵武、程婴就得到众将领的认可。并且，众将领帮着赵武、程婴一起攻打屠岸贾，以报当日屠岸贾屠杀赵氏家族之仇。赵武报仇后，重新得到了祖上原有的全部田邑。

又过了五年，赵武20岁了。一天，程婴对赵武说："当时你全家蒙难时，众多侠义的门客都殉难了，而我没有殉难。不是我不能死，而是我想抚养赵

come to cause trouble because the Zhao family, always helping the king of Jin State to manage state affairs and having made great contributions, were exterminated and people of the whole state felt indignant at the injustice they suffered. Since the divination by the Eight Diagrams showed this, he hoped that the king would take a decision on this matter and rehabilitate the Zhao family. Then Duke Jing of Jin asked: "Does the Zhao family have any descendant alive in the world?" Han Jue then told Duke Jing of Jin that the orphan of Zhao was still alive in the world. Duke Jing of Jin and Han Jue discussed rehabilitating the Zhao family and putting the orphan of Zhao into an important position in the court.

So they secretly brought the orphan of Zhao into the palace. When various generals came into the palace to visit Duke Jing of Jin, Han Jue asked them to meet the orphan of Zhao. The orphan of Zhao was named Zhao Wu. Under the stress of circumstances, various generals said one after another, "The Zhao family were massacred because Tu Angu gave a false order of the king. If not so, how dared we attack the Zhao family? Today, you, the king, want to put the descendant of the Zhao family into an important position. This is exactly what we wish for. We will do whatever you tell us to do."

Thus Zhao Wu and Cheng Ying were recognized by various generals, who helped them attack Tu Angu

氏后人，并让他长大成人。现在你已经长大成人，并且恢复你赵家原有权势，我现在要以死来报答赵盾与公孙杵臼的知遇之恩了。"赵武叩头痛哭："我一辈子都报答不了您的恩情，您怎么忍心抛下我一个人？"程婴坚定地说："我必须死。当时公孙杵臼认为我能担当抚育赵家后代的重任，所以就先死了，如果我不去报知公孙杵臼你已经长大成人的消息，他会以为我没有完成任务呢。"说完，程婴就自尽了。

这就是《史记·赵世家》中所记载的赵氏孤儿的故事，其中所描述的程婴、公孙杵臼、韩厥三人的侠义形象，及其他们所体现的无价友情，让人钦慕不已。

元代（1206—1368）的戏曲作家纪君祥，为这些英雄人物的侠义所感动，加上对无价友情的崇敬，就把这段故事改编为元杂剧《赵氏孤儿》。

纪君祥是元代的戏曲作家，他的生平，我们今天知道的比较少。仅据有限的文献记载，知道他创作有一些戏曲作品，而影响最大的就是《赵氏孤儿》。《赵氏孤儿》的全名是《赵氏孤儿大报仇》，也有说是《冤报冤赵氏孤儿》的，不过人们一般都直接简称

together to avenge his massacre of the Zhao Shuo's family. After the revenge, Zhao Wu obtained all land of his ancestors again.

After another five years, Zhao Wu was 20 years old. One day, Cheng Ying said to Zhao Wu: "When your whole family were confronted by danger, many chivalrous hangers-on died, but I did not die. It was not that I could not die but that I wanted to raise the descendant of the Zhao family and bring him up. Now that you have grown up and restored the power and influence that your family used to have, I want to repay the debt of gratitude for the recognition and appreciation of Zhao Dun and Gongsun Chujiu with death." Zhao Wu kowtowed and cried bitterly: "I cannot repay your kindness in my whole lifetime. How can you bear to leave me alone?" Cheng Ying said resolutely: "I must die. Back then Gongsun Chujiu thought I could shoulder the important task of bringing up the descendant of the Zhao family, so he died first. If I don't tell Gongsun Chujiu that you have grown up, he will think I have not accomplished the task." With these words, Cheng Ying committed suicide.

This is the story of the orphan of Zhao recorded in *Records of the Historian—The House of Zhao*. The chivalrous images of Cheng Ying, Gongsun Chujiu and Han Jue it describes and the priceless friendship they manifested are truly admirable.

为《赵氏孤儿》。

元杂剧,又称作元曲,一般来说,杂剧和散曲合称为元曲,它是元代最重要的文学形式,调子豪壮朴实,用弦乐器伴奏。元杂剧的体制十分严格,一般以"一楔子四折"为一剧,楔子多用于戏剧开始时引出剧情,"折"是按照中国戏剧音乐"宫调"的套数来划分,简单地说来,就是戏剧的场次,每折用若干曲牌组成一个套曲。元杂剧的体制是由关汉卿(生卒年不详)首创的。元杂剧的创作和演出先以元大都(今北京)为中心,后又逐渐流行到南方,至元后期衰

《赵氏孤儿》人物图
The characters of *The Orphan of Zhao*.

Impressed by these chivalrous and heroic figures, Ji Junxiang, a playwright of the Yuan Dynasty (1206–1368), adored the priceless friendship and adapted this story into the Yuan Dynasty *zaju* play *The Orphan of Zhao*.

Ji Junxiang was a playwright of the Yuan Dynasty. His life is little known today. We only know from the records of some literatures that he created some plays, and the most influential one is *The Orphan of Zhao*. The full name of *The Orphan of Zhao* is *The Great Revenge of The Orphan of Zhao*. Some people say it is *Grievance for Grievance, The Orphan of Zhao*, but people generally call it *The Orphan of Zhao* for short.

The *zaju* play of the Yuan Dynasty is also called Yuan Dynasty drama. Generally speaking, the *zaju* play and non-dramatic songs are collectively called the Yuan Dynasty drama. It is an important literary form of the Yuan Dynasty. The tune is grand, heroic and yet plain, accompanied with the music of stringed instruments. The system of the Yuan Dynasty *zaju* play is very strict. Generally, one play consists of "one prologue and four acts." The prologue is mostly for the purpose of introducing the plot of the play at the beginning of the drama; the "acts" are divided according to the cycles of "modes" of Chinese drama music. In simple terms, they are divisions of the drama. In each act, several tunes constitute a cycle of songs. The system of the

落。元杂剧的出现，标志着中国戏曲的成熟，也标志着中国戏剧进入了它的黄金时代。

从我们所了解到的相关情况来看，马约瑟应该是依据明代所编辑刻本的杂剧选集《元曲选》所收入的《赵氏孤儿》来翻译的。因为他只翻译了说白，而没有翻译唱词。《元曲选》中的《赵氏孤儿》是唱词与说白都有的，而现存的元代刻本的《赵氏孤儿》，只有唱词，没有说白。

因为马约瑟翻译的是《元曲选》所收录的《赵氏孤儿》的故事形态。因此，我们要了解纪君祥的《赵氏孤儿》是什么内容，就要依据《元曲选》所收录的《赵氏孤儿》。

纪君祥的《赵氏孤儿》到底讲的是什么故事呢？据《元曲选》所载，它的故事原来是这样的：

《赵氏孤儿》的故事发生在晋灵

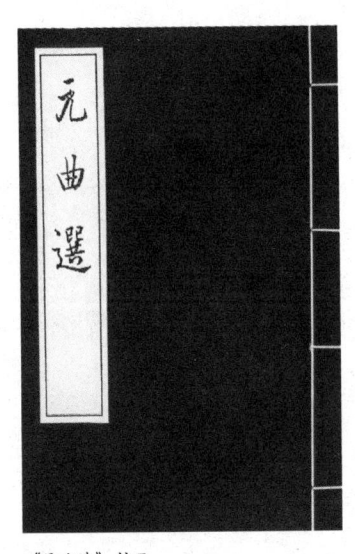

《元曲选》封面
The bookcover of *Selected Yuan Dynasty Dramas*.

《赵氏孤儿大报仇》公孙杵臼唱词
The librettos of Gongsun Chujiu in *The Great Revenge of the Orphan of Zhao*.

Yuan Dynasty *zaju* play was initiated by Guan Hanqing (whose dates are unknown). At first, Dadu of the Yuan Dynasty (present-day Beijing) was the center of creation and performance of Yuan Dynasty *zaju* plays, which later gradually became popular in the south and declined in the late Yuan Dynasty. The emergence of Yuan Dynasty *zaju* plays marked the maturity of Chinese dramas as well as the golden age of Chinese dramas.

In terms of the relevant information we know, Joseph Prémare's translation should be based on *The Orphan of Zhao* in *Selected Yuan Dynasty Dramas*, a block-printed edition of selected *zaju* plays edited in the Ming Dynasty, because he only translated the spoken parts and did not translate the librettos. *The Orphan of Zhao* in *Selected Yuan Dynasty Dramas* has both librettos and spoken parts, while the existing Yuan Dynasty block-printed edition of *The Orphan of Zhao* only has librettos but has no spoken parts.

Because Joseph Prémare translated the story of *The Orphan of Zhao* in *Selected Yuan Dynasty Dramas*, we should take it as the basis to get to know the contents of *The Orphan of Zhao* by Ji Junxiang.

What story does *The Orphan of Zhao* by Ji Junxiang tell? According to *Selected Yuan Dynasty Dramas*, the original story is like this:

The story of *The Orphan of Zhao* took place during the reign of Yigao, Duke Ling of Jin:

公夷皋主政时期。

在《楔子》中，反面人物大臣屠岸贾上场，说是因为他与赵盾"文武不和"，就常常想杀死赵盾。他曾派杀手锄麑去刺杀赵盾。但锄麑感叹赵盾忠君爱民，不忍下手，而自杀，没有杀害赵盾。西戎国进献一只藏獒——非常凶猛的狗。屠岸贾又想出了一条奸计，在家中扎了一个像赵盾的草人，秘密地训练藏獒扑咬这个草人，并让藏獒在这个草人的心脏处找食吃。

一天在大殿上，屠岸贾对晋灵公说："藏獒有灵

《元曲选》中《赵氏孤儿大报仇》插图
Illustrations of *The Great Revenge of the Orphan of Zhao* in *Selected Yuan Dynasty Dramas*.

In the *Prologue*, the villain, minister Tu Angu, appears on the stage. He and Zhao Dun were often at variance because one was a civil official and the other was a military official. Therefore, he often wanted to kill Zhao Dun. He had sent assassin Chuni to assassinate Zhao Dun, but Chuni sighed for Zhao Dun's loyalty to the king and his love for the people and could not bear to do it, so he committed suicide without killing Zhao Dun. The Western Rong State presented a Tibetan mastiff—a very ferocious dog. Tu Angu figured out an evil plot. He made a man of straw at home, secretly trained the Tibetan mastiff to bite it, and had it look for food at its heart.

One day, Tu Angu said to Duke Ling of Jin in the hall: "The Tibetan mastiff is intelligent and can distinguish the virtuous from the wicked. He charges and bites as soon as he sees a wicked person." Tu Angu attempted to let the Tibetan mastiff bite Zhao Dun to death. Zhao Dun's guard Ti Miming could not bear to see Zhao Dun killed, so he killed the Tibetan mastiff. Zhao Dun escaped from the hall in a hurry and ran to his chariot. Actually Tu Angu had sent people to remove a wheel so the chariot could not travel. At that time, Duke Ling of Jin's soldier Ling Zhe who was earlier favored by Zhao Dun used his arm as the wheel, drove horses with one hand, and helped Zhao Dun to escape.

Tu Angu did not give up. He made many malicious

性，能辨忠奸，他一看到奸人就扑咬。"屠岸贾企图让獒咬死赵盾，赵盾的卫士提弥明不忍赵盾被害，出手杀死了藏獒。赵盾急忙逃出大殿，奔上自己的马车。结果马车已经被屠岸贾派人卸下一个车轮，不能行驶。这时，早先曾接受过赵盾恩情的晋灵公甲士灵辄以臂当轮，一手驾马，救赵盾逃走。

屠岸贾仍不死心，就在晋灵公面前说了赵盾的很多坏话，使得晋灵公同意杀死赵氏家族三百余口。由于赵盾的儿子赵朔是晋灵公的驸马，赵朔的妻子怀有身孕，屠岸贾就没敢将其一起杀死。后来屠岸贾假传晋灵公圣旨，逼赵朔自杀，并把赵朔的妻子囚禁在府中。

赵朔自杀前，对妻子交待说："以后若是生下一名男孩，就取小名叫赵氏孤儿，让他长大后为赵家报仇。"

第一折：不久，赵朔的妻子产下一男婴，按照赵朔的遗愿，就取名为赵氏孤儿。屠岸贾知道后，决定待赵氏孤儿满月后再杀死他。屠岸贾派将军韩厥把守府门，以防有人救走赵氏孤儿，并告示全国，有胆敢救赵氏孤儿的，灭其九族。草泽医生程婴是赵盾的门客，与赵盾有着深厚的交情。他去看望赵朔的妻子，

remarks about Zhao Dun in front of Duke Ling of Jin and obtained the Duke's consent to kill more than 300 people of the Zhao family. Because Zhao Dun's son Zhao Shuo was Duke Ling of Jin's son-in-law and Zhao Shuo's wife was pregnant, they were spared death. Later, Tu Angu gave a false imperial decree of Duke Ling of Jin, forced Zhao Shuo to commit suicide, and imprisoned Zhao Shuo's wife in the mansion.

Before committing suicide, Zhao Shuo said to his wife: "If you give birth to a boy, then take the orphan of Zhao as his childhood name and let him avenge the Zhao family when he grows up."

Act One: Before long, Zhao Shuo's wife gave birth to a boy and named him the orphan of Zhao according to Zhao Shuo's last wish. After knowing it, Tu Angu decided to kill the orphan of Zhao when he was one month old. He sent the General Han Jue to guard the mansion gate to prevent anyone from rescuing the orphan of Zhao and announced to all people of the state that should anybody dare to rescue the orphan of Zhao, his whole clan would be exterminated. Cheng Ying, a doctor from the countryside, was Zhao Dun's hanger-on and had deep feelings for Zhao Dun. When he went to visit Zhao Shuo's wife, she asked him to rescue the orphan of Zhao and bring him up to avenge the Zhao family. Cheng Ying was afraid that Zhao Shuo's wife could not bear the interrogation and

赵朔的妻子请求程婴救走赵氏孤儿并把他抚养成人,为赵家报仇。程婴怕赵朔的妻子受不住拷问而说出赵氏孤儿去向,不敢应允。赵朔的妻子为表救子决心,上吊自尽了。程婴赶忙把赵氏孤儿藏到随身带的药箱内,并用一些药材掩盖在赵氏孤儿身上,急急走向府门,欲带赵氏孤儿逃走。走到府门,被在此把守的将军韩厥查知箱内藏有赵氏孤儿。但韩厥也曾受恩于赵家,他也是一位知大礼、明大义的英勇将军,痛恨屠岸贾残害忠良的卑劣行为,也想为救赵氏孤儿出力,于是韩厥放走了程婴。程婴怕韩厥告密,走了三次都折回来,欲让韩厥把他和赵氏孤儿擒住。韩厥知道程婴内心的想法后,拔剑自刎,以坚定程婴救走赵氏孤儿之心。程婴看到韩厥自刎,赶快带着药箱里的赵氏孤儿逃走了。

第二折:屠岸贾得知赵朔妻子和韩厥皆已身亡,而且赵氏孤儿被人救走,恼怒之余,奸计心中生。他再次假传晋灵公圣旨,要把晋国内的满月到半岁大的婴儿全部带到屠府,以验证哪个孩子为赵氏孤儿。他想趁此机会,把每个婴儿都杀死,以实现杀害赵氏孤儿的毒心。程婴救出赵氏孤儿后,直奔太平庄去找公

would tell the orphan of Zhao's whereabouts, so he dared not promise her. To show her resolution to save her son, Zhao Shuo's wife hanged herself. Cheng Ying quickly hid the orphan of Zhao in the medical kit he carried with him, and covered the orphan of Zhao with some medicines. He walked to the mansion gate in a hurry and planned to escape with the orphan of Zhao. When he walked to the mansion gate, General Han Jue, who was on guard, found that the orphan of Zhao was hidden in the medical kit, but he, also a courteous, righteous and valiant general, was once favored by the Zhao family. He detested Tu Angu's vile massacre of the loyal and honest people, and also wanted to do something for the orphan of Zhao. Han Jue let Cheng Ying go. Afraid that Han Jue would tell the secret, Cheng Ying went back three times and wanted Han Jue to arrest him and the orphan of Zhao. After knowing Cheng Ying's thoughts, Han Jue drew his sword and cut his own throat to strengthen Cheng Ying's determination to rescue the orphan of Zhao. Seeing Han Jue cut his throat, Cheng Ying escaped with the orphan of Zhao in the medical kit in a hurry.

Act Two: Tu Angu heard that Zhao Shuo's wife and Han Jue were both dead and that the orphan of Zhao was rescued. Despite his anger, he figured out an evil plot. He gave another false imperial decree of Duke Ling of Jin to bring all babies one to six months old in Jin State to Tu's

伏尔泰与《中国孤儿》

杂剧砖雕，生动刻画了杂剧人物的形态与表情。
Brick engravings of *za ju* scenes, they vividly portray the gestures and expressions of the dramatic figures.

mansion so as to verify which child was the orphan of Zhao. He wanted to seize this opportunity to kill every baby in order to realize the malicious intention of killing the orphan of Zhao. After Cheng Ying rescued the orphan of Zhao, he went directly to Taiping Village to look for Gongsun Chujiu, and asked him to help hide the orphan of Zhao. Gongsun Chujiu was a middle-ranking official in the court before and also a close friend of Zhao Dun. Because the treacherous court official Tu Angu was in power, he could not participate in political affairs and angrily resigned to do farm work in the countryside. Cheng Ying brought the orphan of Zhao to Taiping Village and told Gongsun Chujiu that he wanted him to help hide the orphan of Zhao and that he would go home and disguise his own child less than one month old as the orphan of Zhao. Thus, the orphan of Zhao could be saved and all babies in the state could be spared death. Gongsun Chujiu thought he was already more than 70 years old while Cheng Ying was just 45, so he devised a scheme with Cheng Ying: he let Cheng Ying bring his son less than one month old to his place and disguise him as the orphan of Zhao, and Cheng Ying would bring the real orphan of Zhao home and take him as his own son. Then he let Cheng Ying look for Tu Angu and tell him that the orphan of Zhao was at Gongsun Chujiu's place. Thus, Gongsun Chujiu and Cheng Ying's youngest son would

元代戏台
An opera stage of Yuan Dynasty.

孙杵臼，请他帮助掩藏赵氏孤儿。公孙杵臼原为在朝的中大夫，与赵盾友谊非常深厚。因屠岸贾奸臣掌权，不得参政，怒而辞职，到乡间种田度日。程婴带着赵氏孤儿来到太平庄，告诉公孙杵臼，想让他帮助掩藏赵氏孤儿，自己回家带着自己不满一月的孩子去顶替赵氏孤儿，这样一来可以救下赵氏孤儿，二来可以使全国婴儿免死。公孙杵臼想到自己已经70多岁，而程婴刚刚45岁。就与程婴商量出一条计谋：让程婴把自己不满月的儿子送到他这里来，顶替赵氏孤儿，

be sacrificed to save the orphan of Zhao's life. After the scheme had been devised, Cheng Ying took the orphan of Zhao home in a hurry and sent his youngest son to Gongsun Chujiu's place.

Act Three: Cheng Ying went to Tu Angu's mansion and told him that Gongsun Chujiu was harboring the orphan of Zhao. Tu Angu, an old hand at trickery and deception, terrorized Cheng Ying and asked him why he told on Gongsun Chujiu. Cheng Ying replied that he did so to save the babies of the whole state. Besides, he had a son in his old age and did not want his child less than one month old to be brought to the commander-in-chief's mansion and killed. Otherwise he would die without a son. Tu Angu believed what Cheng Ying said and led the army to surround Taiping Village and capture Gongsun Chujiu. Tu Angu not only cruelly tortured Gongsun Chujiu to force him to surrender the orphan of Zhao, but also asked Cheng Ying to beat up Gongsun Chujiu to see whether Cheng Ying and Gongsun Chujiu were accomplices. Gongsun Chujiu could not bear the horrible torture and killed himself by bumping his head on a step. The soldiers found Cheng Ying's son less than one month old—the fake orphan of Zhao, and Tu Angu cruelly killed him. To reward Cheng Ying, Tu Angu let him become his hanger-on, adopted Cheng Ying's fake son—the real orphan of Zhao, and taught him martial arts.

程婴把真赵氏孤儿抱回家，当作自己儿子。然后让程婴去找屠岸贾，就说赵氏孤儿在公孙杵臼处，这样以牺牲公孙杵臼和程婴的小儿子，来换取赵氏孤儿的性命。计谋定好后，程婴就赶快把赵氏孤儿抱回家，把自己的小儿子送到公孙杵臼处。

第三折：程婴到屠岸贾府上告发说，公孙杵臼窝藏着赵氏孤儿。屠岸贾老奸巨滑，威慑程婴，问他为什么要告发公孙杵臼。程婴回答说，一要救全国婴儿，二是因为自己老年得子，自己的孩儿不满一月，不想被带到帅府杀害，以免绝后。屠岸贾相信了程婴的话，就带军队去围住太平庄，擒拿公孙杵臼。屠岸贾不但对公孙杵臼动用毒刑，逼他交出赵氏孤儿，还再次考验程婴是否与公孙杵臼合伙，让程婴毒打公孙杵臼。公孙杵臼不堪忍受毒刑，撞台阶身亡。士兵搜查到程婴不满月的儿子——假的赵氏孤儿，屠岸贾残忍地把假赵氏孤儿杀死。屠岸贾为了奖励程婴，让程婴作他的门客，并把程婴的假儿子——真的赵氏孤儿——收为义子，传授他武功。

第四折：20年过去，赵氏孤儿已经20岁了。这20年里，他晚上跟随程婴习文，名叫程勃；白天跟随屠

Act Four: After 20 years, the orphan of Zhao was 20 years old. In these years, he studied arts with Cheng Ying and was called Cheng Bo at night, and studied martial arts with Tu Angu and was called Tu Cheng in the daytime. Cheng Ying was well aware of the fact that he was already 65 years old. The orphan of Zhao had grown up, and Cheng Ying must tell him his real identity as well as the history of his family and ask him to avenge his family. From the Tibetan mastiff's chase for Zhao Dun in the court to Gongsun Chujiu's effort to save the orphan of Zhao by bumping his head on a step to kill himself, Cheng Ying drew pictures depicting these events and compiled a book. One day, when Cheng Bo returned after studying martial arts and went to the study to look for Cheng Ying, Cheng Ying left this book compiled by himself for him to read on purpose. After Cheng Bo read it, he was furiously indignant at the vile acts of the man in red but felt confused about the story shown by the pictures in the whole book. He did not know what event these pictures depicted. Cheng Ying explained to Cheng Bo the contents of each picture and in the end told him that Cheng Bo was that orphan of Zhao and that the man in red was his adoptive father Tu Angu. After the orphan of Zhao knew the truth, he swore to kill Tu Angu to avenge his family after reporting to Duke Ling of Jin.

Act Five: The next day, Cheng Bo, the orphan of Zhao,

岸贾习武，名叫屠成。程婴深感自己已经65岁，赵氏孤儿也已长大成人，必须把他的真实身份和他的家族遭遇告诉他，让他为赵氏家族报仇。从赵盾在朝中受藏獒追杀到公孙杵臼为救赵氏孤儿而撞台阶自杀，程婴把这些事情一一绘成图画，编成一本书。一天，程勃习武归来，到书房找程婴，程婴故意把自己编成的这本书留给他看。程勃看过后，为书上穿红衣服的人的残忍行径感到无比气愤，但对整本书中的图画前后所表示的故事感到迷惑不解，不知道这些图画到底在讲述什么事件。程婴为程勃一一讲说每幅图的内容，最后告诉他，程勃就是那个赵氏孤儿，穿红衣服的人就是他的义父屠岸贾。赵氏孤儿知道事实真相后，发誓禀告晋灵公后，杀屠岸贾为自己的家族报仇。

第五折：第二天，赵氏孤儿程勃早朝时向上禀告了他自己的真实身份和要杀屠岸贾报仇的想法。早朝后，晋灵公派上卿魏绛向赵氏孤儿程勃传旨，称屠岸贾拥兵太重，为防生变，程勃可以在私下里捉拿屠岸贾。程勃领旨后，匹马单枪于闹市中专门等候屠岸贾经过。不久屠岸贾带着一队人马，要返回其私宅。程勃看到后，催马向前，向屠岸贾质问的同时，三下五

reported his real identity and his intention of killing Tu Angu for revenge during the morning court. After the morning court, Duke Ling of Jin sent senior minister Wei Jiang to give a decree to the orphan of Zhao, saying that because Tu Angu had too many soldiers, Cheng Bo could capture Tu Angu secretly to prevent trouble. After receiving the decree, Cheng Bo waited for Tu Angu to come in the busy commercial area alone. Before long, Tu Angu led a team of soldiers to return to his private house. When Cheng Bo saw them, he urged the horse on. While interrogating Tu Angu, Cheng Bo captured him at one go. At that time, Cheng Ying also came for fear of something unexpected. The two of them escorted Tu Angu to Wei Jiang's mansion. Wei Jiang decided to execute Tu Angu and read Duke Ling of Jin's decree: Cheng Bo, the orphan of Zhao, was allowed to have the surname of Zhao and inherit the Zhao family's original title of nobility and was given the name of Zhao Wu; Han Jue's descendant would still be a senior general; Cheng Ying was to be rewarded with ten *qing* of country estate to commend his brave act of saving the orphan of Zhao; a stele and tomb were to be built for Gongsun Chujiu and he was to be buried with full honors; the brave acts of Ti Miming, Ling Zhe were also commended. The whole story ended with the punishment of the villain and the commendation of righteous people.

伏尔泰与《中国孤儿》

京剧《赵氏孤儿》剧照
A stage photo of the Peking opera *The Orphan of Zhao*.

除二地就把屠岸贾擒住了。这时，程婴怕程勃出现意外，也赶来了。他们两人就把屠岸贾押到魏绛府里。魏绛决定把屠岸贾处死。魏绛宣读了晋灵公的旨意：让赵氏孤儿程勃复姓赵，并赐名为赵武，荫袭赵家原来的爵位；韩厥的后代仍然继为上将；赏赐给程婴十顷田庄，以表扬拯救赵氏孤儿的英勇行为；给公孙杵臼立碑造墓，进行厚葬；对提弥明、灵辄等人的英勇

From the synopsis of Ji Junxiang's *The Orphan of Zhao*, we can see that Ji Junxiang added his own artistic fabrications on the basis of the story provided in the *Records of the Historian—The House of Zhao* to make the whole story more complete and suspenseful. The ideas of poetic justice, commendation of the righteous and "a gentleman who is ready to die for his bosom friends" penetrate the exciting development of the story.

Maybe the Europeans admired deeply such Confucian ideas contained in *The Orphan of Zhao* and the chivalrous spirit manifested by Gongsun Chujiu, Cheng Ying, Han Jue, etc., so Joseph Prémare took the trouble to translate it into French. But perhaps he never thought that his translation of *The Orphan of Zhao* would greatly shock the French drama circles and even the European drama circles, it was the great French thinker, writer and playwright Voltaire who played the main role.

行为，也予以奖赏。整个故事在恶人受惩、仁人义士受褒扬的结局中结束。

通过纪君祥《赵氏孤儿》的故事梗概，我们可以看出，纪君祥在《史记·赵世家》所提供的故事基础上，增加了一些自己的艺术虚构，把整个故事讲述得更加完整、更加具有悬念，在扣人心弦的故事发展中，将扬善惩恶、褒奖仁义、"士为知己者死"的观念渗透于其中。

也许正是《赵氏孤儿》中所蕴涵的这种儒家思想观念，及公孙杵臼、程婴、韩厥等人身上所体现的侠义精神，令欧洲人深为欣赏，马约瑟不辞辛苦地把它翻译成法语。不过也许他自己也没有想到，他翻译的《赵氏孤儿》，竟然引起了法国戏剧界乃至欧洲戏剧界的一场巨大的震动。在这场震动中，起着主要作用的正是法国大思想家、文学家、戏剧家伏尔泰。

Guan Hanqing

Guan Hanqing, the most important writer of Yuan Dynasty *zaju* plays, was active in northern China in the 13th century and mainly lived in Dadu of the Yuan Dynasty (present-day Beijing). He created more than 60 plays in his lifetime, and more than ten were handed down. At present, *The Injustice to Dou E*, *The Riverside Pavilion* and *Meeting the Enemies Alone* are still performed on the drama stage. In 1958, Guan Hanqing was nominated by World Peace Council as a world cultural celebrity; *Britannica Concise Encyclopedia* calls him "the greatest Chinese playwright generally acknowledged by literary criticism circles;" at present, his plays have been translated into many languages including English, French, German, Japanese.

Selected Yuan Dynasty Dramas

Also called *100 Dramas of the Yuan Dynasty*, it is a collection of Yuan Dynasty *zaju* plays compiled by Zang Maoxun (1550–1620) of the Ming Dynasty, including 100 plays: 94 Yuan Dynasty *zaju* plays and six Ming Dynasty *zaju* plays. Most plays were edited by Zang Maoxun with complete actions and spoken parts as well as voice annotations. It played an important role in the spreading of Yuan Dynasty *zaju* plays and was widely read. Yuan Dynasty *zaju* play researchers usually take this book as the basis.

关汉卿

关汉卿是元杂剧最重要的作者,他活动于13世纪的中国北方,以元大都(即今天的北京)为主要居住地。他一生创作了60多部剧本,传世的有十多部,至今仍在戏剧舞台上演出的则有《窦娥冤》、《望江亭》和《单刀会》。关汉卿在1958年曾被世界和平理事会提名为"世界文化名人",《英国简明百科全书》称他为"文艺理论界公认的中国最伟大的戏剧家",目前他的剧作已被翻译成英、法、德、日等多国文字。

《元曲选》

又名《元人百种曲》,元杂剧剧本集。明代臧懋循(1550—1620)编,其中收录元代杂剧94种,明代杂剧6种,总计100种。剧本大多经过臧氏加工整理,科白完整,并附有音注。它对元代杂剧的传播起了重要作用,一般研究元杂剧者多以此书为依据,流传较广。

III

The Orphan of China by Voltaire

Voltaire, alias Francois Marie Arouet, was born into an affluent family on November 21, 1694, in Paris, nicknamed the "city of flowers." When Voltaire was born, he was weak and had a poor physical condition. His parents were no longer young and this meant much trouble and problem for his parents. His nanny always said to his parents: "This boy cannot live long." However, Voltaire did not die young as his nanny had predicted, and instead, he vigorously struggled and fought against the backward social systems and religious oppression for 84 years.

Although Voltaire was physically weak, he was exceptionally smart. When he was three years old, he could recite a long poem by Lud, an agnostic. That was the first French poem against religions. Maybe it was this poem that helped Voltaire to build the base of his personality to detest the blind religious craze and to oppose the authority when he grew up.

3

伏尔泰的《中国孤儿》

伏尔泰像
A portrait of Voltaire.

  伏尔泰，原名弗朗索瓦·玛丽·阿鲁埃，1694年11月21日，出生在素有"花都"之称的法国巴黎，一个比较富裕的家庭。伏尔泰刚刚出生时，身体状况非常差，而他的父母年龄都已经很大，这为他的父母带来了很大烦恼。他的保姆经常对他的父母预言说："这个孩子活不过一个小时了。"不过，伏尔泰并没有像他的保姆所预言的那样，他轰轰烈烈地与落后的社会制度、宗教压迫斗争了84年。

  伏尔泰虽然天生体弱，但智力超群。他三岁时，就能背诵《摩西亚特》长诗。这首长诗由不可知论者卢德创作，是法国第一首公开攻击宗教的诗篇。也许

When Voltaire was seven years old, his mother died. His father then had to assume full responsibility for his education. His father wanted to train him into a talent so that he would be able to make his way to the rank of aristocrats. When Voltaire was 10, he was sent by his father to Louis-le-Grand middle school run by the Society of Jesus, and this was a school for the children of aristocrats. In this school, he not only learned theology, but also Greek, Latin, rhetoric, poetry, medicine, history, drama and protocols and etiquette of the upper class. During this period, Voltaire's gift in literature was fully demonstrated. When he was 12, he, based on an ancient Roman legend, wrote the tragedy *Amullius and Numitore*. His gift in literature creation was not only widely praised by the teachers, but was also appreciated by Mrs. Ninon, a cultural celebrity in Paris then. Appreciating his excellent poems, Mrs. Ninon gave him 2,000 livre (a currency unit then in Paris) so that he could buy books.

In Louis-le-Grand middle school, he had the chance to read some books advocating liberal thoughts, and became very much interested in these books which were mainly read by the adults, in particular, works by philosopher Pierre Bell. His works were full of the spirit to be doubtful of the world and to challenge bravely the religious craze and dogma. This made a far-reaching impact on the young Voltaire and made him unruly and ready to declare

正是这首长诗，奠定了伏尔泰长大后厌恶盲目的宗教狂热并勇敢与权威抗争的性格基础。

伏尔泰七岁时，母亲去世。教育他的重担完全落在了父亲身上。他的父亲一心想把他培养成才，以期能跻身于贵族行列。伏尔泰十岁时，就被父亲送到了耶稣会主办的圣路易中学学习，这是一所为贵族子弟办的学校。在这里，他不仅学习神学，还学习希腊文、拉丁文、修辞学、诗学、医学、历史、戏剧和各种上流社会的礼仪。伏尔泰在此学习期间，他的文学天赋得到充分体现。12岁时，他就根据古罗马传说写成了悲剧《阿穆利乌斯和努弥托耳》。他的创作才能不仅得到了老师的普遍称赞，也得到了当时巴黎的文化名人尼侬夫人的赏识。尼侬夫人曾因他优秀的诗作，而赠与他2000利弗尔（巴黎当时的货币单位），让他购买图书。

在圣路易中学，他接触到一些宣传自由思想的图书，并且对这些只有成人才阅读的图书产生了极大的阅读兴趣。特别是哲学家毕耶尔·贝尔的著作。他的著作中洋溢着的怀疑世事与大举向宗教狂热和宗教教义挑战的精神，对年轻的伏尔泰产生了深刻影响，使

war against all inhumane rules and bylaws. During this period, he often took part in the gathering of a liberal group "Pantheon Group," criticized the government and exposed errors and problems of the times. His talent in literary creation helped win him a big influence in the liberal group. Because he was good at writing poems to satirize, the members of this liberal group praised him as an "anti-government poet." From then on, he embarked on a road to fighting against the power and authority.

In the course of fighting against the power and authority in France, Voltaire created numerous works to express and preach his ideas and awake the French public to resist and fight against the dark religions and government. For example, on September 1, 1715, Louis XIV died and Louis XV, who was only five years old, was enthroned. Duke of Orleans then assisted the young king to manage the government affairs. Duke of Orleans lived a corrupt and dissipated life and even had affairs with his daughter. He also traded official ranks for money, making the political and government system of France corrupt. Dissatisfied and angry with the dark social reality, Voltaire wrote, in the spring of 1717, his satirical poem *Puerorgnante*. This poem began with a seven-year-old French king and then mentioned the Duke of Orleans, satirized the king and the Duke of Orleans, and ended with the line saying "France will die." This poem made

得其桀骜不驯、狂放成性，想向一切缺乏人性的规章制度宣战。在此期间，他经常参加"圣殿集团"的聚会，批评朝政，针砭时弊。他的文学创作才能，使得他在"圣殿集团"内有着较大影响。由于他善于即兴创作讽刺诗，被"圣殿集团"的成员称赞为"反政府诗人"，从此一发而不可收拾，开始了他与强权斗争的一生。

在伏尔泰与法国强权作斗争的过程中，他创作了众多的作品，以宣扬他的理念，唤醒法国民众，起来反抗当时法国黑暗的宗教与政府统治。如在1715年9月1日，路易十四去世，年仅5岁的路易十五继位。奥尔良公爵辅助幼主管理朝政。奥尔良公爵本人生活糜烂荒淫，曾与自己的女儿私通，且卖官鬻爵，使得法国政治一片黑暗。不满黑暗社会现实的伏尔泰，于1717年春天，创作了讽刺诗《幼主》。这首诗从7岁的法国国王谈起，继而涉及到奥尔良公爵，对国王和奥尔良公爵进行了无情的讽刺，并以"法国将要灭亡"结束全诗。这首诗使得奥尔良公爵非常震怒，伏尔泰被投进了巴士底狱。

牢狱之灾不仅没有阻碍伏尔泰的斗志，反而激发

巴士底狱
The Bastille.

the Duke of Orleans furious, and Voltaire was put in the Bastille prison.

The imprisonment did not oppress Voltaire's will to fight; instead, it triggered off even greater indignation towards the oppression in the society and rekindled his enthusiasm to create more works. In the year while he was imprisoned in the Bastille, he completed the play *Oedipe*. After he was released from the Bastille, the first

油画《俄狄浦斯与斯芬克斯》
A painting entitled Oedipus and the Sphinx.

了他对社会压制的愤慨，助长了他的创作激情。被监禁在巴士底狱将近一年的时间里，他不仅创作了大量反映不满社会不平等的诗作，而且完成了《俄狄浦斯》的创作。他出狱后，第一件事就是想办法出版《俄狄浦斯》，并且首次使用"伏尔泰"作为笔名。1718年11月18日，《俄狄浦斯》得以在巴黎的法兰西喜剧院首次公演，得到了观众的普遍认可与赞誉，连续上演了45场，场场爆满。这部悲剧的成功，完全是得益于伏尔泰在此剧作中所蕴藏的反抗命运、揭示神与宗教的欺骗性的深刻内涵。这种针砭社会现实的精神，契合了广大观众的内心企求。如他借俄狄浦斯之口说出："残酷的神啊，我的罪孽完全是你们造成的，而你们却要根据这些罪孽把我处

thing he did was to have *Oedipe* published, and for the first time, he used his pen name "Voltaire." On November 18, 1718, *Oedipe* made its debut at Comedie-Francaise (Theatre Francais). The play immediately won wide recognition and praises from the audiences, and was staged consecutively for 45 times to a packed audience. The success of this tragedy was fully attributable to the spirit of resistance against fate and to the revelation of the fraudulence of the gods and religion in this play. This spirit of satirizing the social realities matched well with the inner desire of the audiences. For example, through the mouth of Oedipus, he said: "My merciless god, you are the source of my sins, but you are to put me to death based on these sins." This was what everyone who was not willing to be subjected to the oppression of the rulers and religion wanted to say but dared not to speak out. Voltaire spoke out for them, so they were willing to watch *Oedipe*.

Voltaire did not stop his fight against the hypocritical and dark religions till his death. On May 30, 1778, when Voltaire was critically ill and at the door of death, the priest asked him: "My child, do you acknowledge the divinity of Jesus Christ? Voltaire remained silent without uttering a single word, and the priest asked this question repeatedly. Voltaire, who was dying, suddenly shouted to the priest: "Let me die quietly and peacefully!" After the

死。"这是每位不甘于受统治者和宗教压迫的人想说而又不敢说的心声。伏尔泰替他们说出来了，他们当然乐意于观看《俄狄浦斯》的上演。

伏尔泰至死也没有停止与虚伪、黑暗的宗教作斗争。1778年5月30日，伏尔泰生命垂危，弥留之际，神甫问他："我的孩子，您承认耶稣基督的神性吗？"面对沉默不言的伏尔泰，神甫反复追问。奄奄一息的伏尔泰突然大声呵斥道："让我安静地去死吧！"说完之后，溘然长眠。

可以说伏尔泰的一生，是与强权、宗教统治斗争的一生。他斗争的武器就是他所创作的大量的哲学、文学与戏剧等作品，特别是戏剧作品，充分宣扬了他的观念。

翻看他的诸多著作，可以发现，他在近80部作品、200多封书信中提到并赞扬中国。为何他会有如此表现，原来是因为他从中国的传统文化中找到了斗争的精神武器。他几乎对于中国的一切都深为叹服，认为中国就是他的理想国。他对中国的孔子（约前551—前479，中国古代著名的思想家、教育家，儒家学派创始人）更是崇敬有加，认为"孔子是真正的圣人"，

words, Voltaire died.

The life of Voltaire was characterized by his unremitting fight against the power and religious rule. His weapon was his works on philosophy, literature and plays, and especially the plays through which he advocated and preached his ideas.

Reading his works, it could be found that he, in about 80 works and more than 200 letters, mentioned and praised China. Why did he do this? The reason was that he found his spiritual weapon for the fight from the Chinese traditional culture. He admired virtually anything from China, and considered China as his Utopia. He highly admired Confucius (c. 551–479 BC, ancient Chinese philosopher, educator and founder the Confucianism school), and deemed "Confucius as the real saint," "Moses of the mankind, and that no other lawgivers could have declared truth and gospel more useful to the world than Confucius did," and "an ancient sage, about 600 years before the founding of the Christianity, who instructed the offspring to follow and defend the virtues." He also highly admired the thoughts and philosophy of Confucius. He said that Confucius's "every quotation is related to the happiness of the mankind," and "if everyone follows and abides by his words, there will not be any war or fight on the globe." His admiration for Confucius was from his heart. In his studio, a portrait of Confucius was hanging

孔子像
A portrait of Confucius.

"人类的立法者,没有任何立法者比孔夫子曾对世界宣布了更有用的真理","孔子是一位在基督教创立之前约600年教导后辈谨守美德的先贤古哲"。他对孔子的思想更是佩服得五体投地,他说孔子的"每一条语录都关系到人类的幸福","倘若人人以此自律,地球上就再也不会有争斗了"。他对孔子的这种赞颂,深入到了他的骨子里,他在工作室内悬挂着一幅孔子的画像,天天顶礼膜拜。

　　伏尔泰对于孔子的崇拜,并不仅限于孔子个人,而是对以孔子为代表的儒家思想的认同。他在对中国文化深思后发现,儒家思想在中国历史进程中起着不可替代的作用。正是儒学,使中国人养成了善良、宽容、淳朴、重信用的品质和以孝为先的人生准则。这一切,在伏尔泰看来,在当时的法国甚至欧洲是多么的匮乏,特别是中国的国君受到儒学的影响,也是那

and he worshipped Confucius everyday.

Voltaire not only admired Confucius, but his admiration also reflected his recognition of the Confucian thinking represented by Confucius. He, after pondering over the Chinese culture, found that the Confucianism played an irreplaceable role in the history of China. It was Confucianism that helped the Chinese to nurture such traits as kindness, tolerance and trustworthiness and their code of conduct for life highlighting filial piety. These, in the eye of Voltaire, were what France, even Europe, was then lacking of. In particular, the Chinese emperors, influenced by the Confucianism, were also very witty, benevolent and were full of philosophical thoughts. Voltaire desperately hoped that the king of France would also, like the Chinese emperors, have the wisdom to rule the country and be kind and benevolent to their people.

When Voltaire read *The Orphan of Zhao, a Chinese Tragedy* translated by Ma Yuese, he also found the "Chinese spirit" that he recognized and admired and was deeply moved by the story of sacrificing life for love and friendship. He then decided to adapt this story into the form widely accepted by the French audiences to advocate the philosophy contained in this story. Due to various factors, however, Voltaire did not immediately start to adapt *The Orphan of Zhao*. He did not start the adaptation till the 1750s.

When it came to why he delayed his plan and then

么的睿智、仁慈而富有哲学思想。伏尔泰非常希望法国的国君也能像中国的国君一样，有治理国家的英明和对待人民的宽厚。

当伏尔泰读到马约瑟翻译的《中国悲剧〈赵氏孤儿〉》，更是于其中找到了他所认同的"中国精神"，深深为这种重情重谊而不惜生命的故事所感动，并决定把这个故事改编成法国观众所能接受的形式，来宣扬故事中所蕴涵的哲理。由于多种原因，当时的伏尔泰并

明代《圣迹图》（局部），描绘了孔子周游列国、退修诗书、教授弟子的生活片段。
The Holy Trace (detail), Ming Dynasty, depicts the dribs and drabs of Confucius touring the kingdoms, receding and mending the works, and teaching his disciples.

suddenly started to adapt it, we have to mention Jean-Jacques Rousseau (1712–1778, renowned French enlightenment thinker, philosopher, educator and litterateur, the ideology forerunner of the French Revolution in the 18th century, and one of the major figures of the Enlightenment Movement). To a great extent, it was Rousseau who spurred Voltaire to materialize his plan. Then, how did Rousseau promote Voltaire to adapt *The Orphan of Zhao*? This began with their different attitudes towards China.

As mentioned above, Voltaire considered anything from and about China as beautiful and perfect and considered China as one of the few Utopian states in the world. When Voltaire regarded China so highly, he would naturally spare no effort in praising and extolling China and the Chinese civilization, and would not tolerate any bad words or criticism about the nation. Different from Voltaire, Rousseau was not a "fan" of China or the Chinese civilization. He not only saw China from a dialectic point of view, but also sometimes rejected China and its culture, and made some criticism about it.

In 1750 when Voltaire was highly praising and extolling China's ancient civilization and progress, Rousseau wrote an article, in which he denounced China's science, technology and civilization, and sent a copy of this article to Voltaire to show his attitude towards China. This

卢梭像
A portrait of Rousseau.

没有能够立即着手改编《赵氏孤儿》。而直到18世纪50年代，他才真正开始改编工作。

至于他为什么拖到此时而突然进行改编，我们就不能不说到卢梭（让·雅各·卢梭，1712—1778，是法国著名启蒙思想家、哲学家、教育家、文学家，是18世纪法国大革命的思想先驱，启蒙运动最卓越的代表人物之一。）因为很大程度上，是卢梭促使伏尔泰实现了他的想法。卢梭怎么会促使伏尔泰对《赵氏孤儿》进行改编呢？这事还得从他们两人对待中国的态度说起。

如前所述，伏尔泰认为中国的一切都那么美好、毫无瑕疵，完全是世界上少见的理想国度。伏尔泰既然这样认为，他当然就会不遗余力地称赞、颂扬中国和中国文明，同样也不想听到别人说中国的坏话。与伏尔泰不同，卢梭可不是一位中国和中国文明的"铁杆粉丝"，他不仅用辩证的眼光看待中国，而且有时甚至会抵制中国和中国文化，针对中国提出一些批评。

made Voltaire very angry. So he decided to fight back and wanted to prove the advantages of China's ancient civilization and its outstanding customs. At this moment, he recalled *The Orphan of Zhao, a Chinese Tragedy*, translated by Ma Yuese, which he read several years ago, and he believed that this story was a perfect manifestation of the Chinese customs and spirit. Under such circumstances, he decided to execute his plan, and started to adapt Ji Junxiang's *The Orphan of Zhao* translated by Ma Yuese, so as to refute Rousseau's claims and to advocate the "Chinese spirit."

Voltaire had such comments on *The Orphan of Zhao*: "*The Orphan of Zhao* is a valuable masterpiece. It could help people to better understand the Chinese spirit, play a role greater than any statements or descriptions about this empire ever made or to be made." Then, what was the "Chinese spirit" mentioned by Voltaire? In *The Orphan of Zhao*, Voltaire found that persons as Ti Miming, Ling Zhe, Han Jue, Gongsun Chujiu and Cheng Ying were ready to sacrifice their lives in order to protect the orphan of the Zhao family, and their action showed their cherishment of integrity, friendship, loyalty and chivalry, and manifested the doctrines of Confucius. This cherishment of the state, sacrifice and justice was the "Chinese spirit" as understood by Voltaire.

Voltaire also noticed that the times in which Ji Junxiang,

1750年，在伏尔泰极力称赞中国的古老文明与进步时，卢梭写了一篇文章，极大地贬斥了中国的科学技术与文明，并且他还把这篇文章送给伏尔泰，以表明自己对待中国的态度。这让伏尔泰非常生气，他决定对卢梭予以还击，证明中国古老文明的优越性和优秀的风俗。于是，他就想到了若干年前看到的马约瑟翻译的《中国悲剧〈赵氏孤儿〉》，它的故事不正可以说明中国风俗与中国精神吗？！就这样，他决定实现自己的愿望，对马约瑟翻译的纪君祥的《赵氏孤儿》进行改编，驳斥卢梭，宣扬"中国精神"。

对于《赵氏孤儿》，伏尔泰曾这样评论："《赵氏孤儿》是一篇宝贵的大作，它使人了解中国精神，有甚于人们对这个大帝国所曾作和所将作的一切陈述。"到底什么是伏尔泰所说的"中国精神"呢？原来，伏尔泰在《赵氏孤儿》中，看到提弥明、灵辄、韩厥、公孙杵臼、程婴等人为了保护赵氏孤儿，不惜牺牲宝贵的生命，体现出重气节、讲情义、明大理的侠气，以实际行动诠释了孔子学说。这种以国家为重、舍己救人、伸张正义，就是伏尔泰所理解的"中国精神"。

the author of *The Orphan of Zhao*, lived was the age when the minority ethnic—the Mongols moved southwards to control and rule the central China. However, after the Mongols established the Yuan Dynasty and ruled China, the culture of central China and the Confucianism were not affected, and on the contrary, the old barbarism and living habits of the Mongols were completely submitted to the culture of central China and the doctrines of Confucianism. On this, Voltaire said: "This play was written in the 14th century—the dynasty of Genghis Khan. This is another evidence to prove that the Tartary conquerors could not change the customs of the ethnic groups lost in the wars. They assumed the responsibility of protecting all arts and culture established in China, and they accepted all rules already set." The story of *The Orphan of Zhao* "showed the advantages of sense and talent over ignorance and barbarian violence; furthermore, the Tartars had served as evidence to this twice, because when they again conquered this huge empire at the beginning of the last century, they once again surrendered to the culture and virtues of the losers in the war, the peoples of the two states constituted one nationality, and it was ruled with the oldest legal system in the world." Because Voltaire had noticed so many points constructive to advocating his ideas and doctrines in the play *The Orphan of Zhao*, he decided to adapt the play to serve as

伏尔泰与《中国孤儿》

成吉思汗像
A portrait of Genghis Khan.

　　伏尔泰还看到，《赵氏孤儿》的作者纪君祥所处的时代，是少数民族——蒙古族入主中原的时代。但是，以蒙古族为统治核心的元朝建立后，并没有使得中原文化、儒家学说受到破坏，相反，蒙古族固有的野蛮与蒙昧和陈旧的生活习俗，完全地臣伏于中原文化、儒家学说。关于这一点，伏尔泰说："这个剧本创作于14世纪，就是在成吉思汗朝。这又是一个新的证据，证明鞑靼的胜利者不能改变战败民族的风俗。他们保护着在中国建立起来的一切艺术，他们接受它的一切法规。"《赵氏孤儿》的故事"说明理性与天才对盲目、野蛮的暴力所具有的优越性；而且鞑靼已经两次提供这个例证了，因为当他们上世纪初又征服了这个庞大帝国的时候，他们再度降服于战败者的文德下；两国人民只构成了一个民族，由世界上最古老的法制治理着"。伏尔泰正是于《赵氏孤儿》剧本身上看到了这么多的有益于他观点宣扬的因素，才在反驳

99

a weapon for argument with Rousseau when he was to refute Rousseau's claims on China.

Voltaire admired Confucius and his doctrine, and he repeatedly stated this point in his works. In the adaptation of *The Orphan of Zhao*, he continued to do so, and more significantly, he even pondered the possibility of directly including the role of Confucius in the play so as to show the process how the Confucianism and civilization conquered the valiant and barbaric Tartars. Although he did not do so in the adaptation, he added the subtitle "Five-act Confucian Doctrine Play" to the play *The Orphan of China*, so as to indicate the relationship of this play with Confucius and his doctrine.

The story of *The Orphan of China* adapted by Voltaire was different with that of *The Orphan of Zhao* written by Ji Junxiang. *The Orphan of China* had five acts and its story was like this:

Act I

Idame, the heroine, and her servant Asseli appeared on stage. Idame told Asseli that her former lover was named Genghis Khan, and Genghis Khan once proposed to her but she refused. Later, she married Zamti. In the imperial court, the emperor handed the newly-born crown prince over to Zamti, asked him to raise the crown prince, ordered him to lead the army to defeat the enemies and restore the state. Zamti had to find a safe and secure

卢梭的中国观时,选择了改编《赵氏孤儿》,作为他与卢梭论辩的武器。

伏尔泰非常崇拜孔子及其学说,他总是不断地在他的作品中表明这一点。在对《赵氏孤儿》的改编中,他依然如此,并且更为明显的是,他开始想直接让孔子本人出现在剧中,以展现儒学与文明战胜彪悍而野蛮的鞑靼人的过程。尽管后来他并没有这样做,不过还是把他改编而成的《中国孤儿》加上"五幕孔子道德戏"的副标题,以表明此剧作与孔子及其道德学说的关系。

伏尔泰改编而成的《中国孤儿》,所讲述的故事与纪君祥的《赵氏孤儿》相比,已经有了许多不同。《中国孤儿》共分五幕,所讲的

伏尔泰《中国孤儿》1755年上演时,剧中演员扮演的成吉思汗。
Kublai Khan impersonated by the actor in drama *The Orphan of China*.

method to hide the crown prince so as to avoid possible killing.

Shortly afterwards, the imperial court was attacked and seized by the army led by Genghis Khan, and the emperor and the royal family members were killed. Because Zamti had already sent his servant Etan to properly hide the crown prince, he was not slaughtered. But Octar, the commander of the Genghis Khan army, ordered people to surrender the crown prince, the heir to the royal throne, and threatened that whoever dared to hide the crown prince, he and his entire family would be slaughtered. Zamti and Etan discussed how they could protect and save the crown prince. Zamti intended to sacrifice his only son by handing over him as the crown prince so as to save the life of the crown prince. He prayed to the heaven and hoped the God would bless the crown prince.

Act II

Zamti was, in his heart, unwilling to sacrifice his son, and imagined various miserable scenes when his son was to be killed. He told Etan to keep this secret from his wife, and not to let her know that he had to pass his son as crown prince. Unfortunately, his words were overheard by his wife. She was very angry, and said she would not let her own son be slaughtered even if she herself was to die for that. She desperately held her son tightly. At this moment, Octar, leading a group of soldiers, arrived, and

故事是这样的：

第一幕

女主角易达迷和女仆阿赛利出场。易达迷告诉阿赛利，她原来有一个恋人叫铁木真，铁木真曾向她求婚，但她没有答应他。后来，她就嫁给了扎迷惕。在宫中，皇帝把刚出生的太子交给扎迷惕，让他把太子抚养成人，带领众将，打败敌人，恢复故国。

不久，皇宫被铁木真的军队攻破，皇帝和皇族都被杀害。由于扎迷惕早先已经派仆人额坦把小太子藏好，小太子躲过一劫。但铁木真军队的大首领窝阔台要求人们交出这位皇位继承人，并说谁要是敢藏匿皇太子，就会被灭九族。扎迷惕和额坦商量，应该如何掩护、拯救皇太子，扎迷惕想让自己的独生子冒充皇太子，想用自己儿子的死来拯救皇太子。

第二幕

扎迷惕内心深处也舍不得自己的儿子，幻想着儿子将要被处死的种种惨状。他告诉额坦，不要让他的妻子知道他要用自己的儿子来冒充皇太子。但他的话恰好被他的妻子听到了，她非常恼怒，说即使自己去死，也不能让儿子去送死。她拼命地抱着自己的儿子

demanded them to surrender the crown prince as soon as possible. Zamti pretended to follow his order, and said he would soon find the crown prince and hand him over. His wife, now unable to do anything to save her own son, handed over her son. Genghis Khan met Octar, and gave the order to kill the crown prince only and not to slay others.

When Genghis Khan was with Octar, he sadly recalled and narrated his past and his first love. He wanted very much to see his first love again and to stay together with her. However, Octar did not understand the words from the bottom of Genghis Khan's heart, and just echoed to Genghis Khan pretentiously. At this moment, Osman, a general of Genghis Khan, came and reported to Genghis Khan: When the crown prince was to be executed, a furious woman arrived and said the one to be slaughtered was her son, not the crown prince.

Act III

Genghis Khan was very angry, and issued an order to thoroughly investigate into the matter. At this moment, a guard escorted the woman to Genghis Khan. At the first glance of this woman, he was completely shocked. He recognized that this woman was his first love, whom he had been thinking and dreaming of day and night, and he could hardly believe this. He ordered the guards to release the infant and not to make trouble with this woman, and

不撒手。这时，窝阔台带着一队人马赶到，要求人们赶快交出皇太子。扎迷惕假装惟命是从，说他很快就会找到皇太子交给他们。他的妻子在百般无奈之下，松手交出了自己的儿子。铁木真见到窝阔台，命令他只处死皇太子就行了，不用杀害其他的人。

铁木真和窝阔台单独在一起，他非常伤感地叙述了他的过去、他的初恋。他非常渴望能够再见到他的初恋情人，能够与初恋情人在一起。但是，铁木真的肺腑之言，粗鲁的窝阔台并不能听懂，他只是随声附和铁木真。这时，铁木真的将官兀思蛮来报说，正当准备处死皇太子的时候，一名大发雷霆的女子呼喊着说大家要杀死的是她的亲生儿子，不是皇太子。

第三幕

铁木真非常生气，降旨要查清整件事。这时，校尉把那个女子押解到他面前。铁木真看了一眼，感到万分震惊。他认出这个女子正是让他日思夜想的初恋情人，他几乎不敢相信这是事实。他要求士兵放了那个婴儿，也不要为难这个女子，铁木真责令扎迷惕弥补其过，赶快交出真的皇太子，否则就要被处死。

铁木真带着窝阔台回府，他再次向窝阔台倾诉衷

what he wanted was to have the crown prince killed.

Genghis Khan ordered Idame to remedy her wrongdoings and deliver the real crown prince as soon as possible; otherwise she would be executed.

Genghis Khan was very angry and returned to his palace with Octar. Again, he revealed what had been hidden in his heart, and said how dearly he loved his first sweetheart. At this moment, Osman came again, and said that woman and her husband Zamti were to commit suicide together. Genghis Khan said hurriedly that he wanted them to live and did not want that woman to die. He told Octar that anything could be done to save that woman's life.

Act IV

Octar tried hard to persuade Genghis Khan to kill Idame, but Genghis Khan was not deluded by him, because he admired the people from central China. He said, to the people from central China, "You don't have any means to make them bow down or falter. What can I say? The more I see, the more must I admire. This wondrous people have a long history and a large population, and they are so great in arts and arms. Their kings on the basis of wisdom founded all their power and authority. They enacted national laws, and governed by virtue and without conquest. But the heaven bestowed on us nothing but force. Our only art is cruel war; our

肠，说他是如何深爱着昔日的恋人。这时，兀思蛮又来报，说那个女子准备与他的丈夫扎迷惕一起自杀。铁木真急忙告诉窝阔台，无论如何都要让那个女子活下来。

第四幕

窝阔台极力地鼓动铁木真杀死扎迷惕，但铁木真没有受他的蛊惑，因为他心中钦佩中原人。他说，中原人，"没有任何办法能使他们屈服，没有任何办法能使他们颤抖。我该说什么呢？如果我密切注意到了这个遭到蹂躏和沦陷的民族。尽管我不愿意，我还是崇拜他们，却又为他们带上了桎梏，我发现其著作教育了全天下。我看到了一个历史悠久、手艺精巧和人数众多的民族。其国干以智慧为其势力的基础，以其已归附邻居为幸运的立法者，不用征服而统治和由风俗习惯行使政权。上天只赐给我们天生的力量，我们的艺术就是战争，摧毁是我们的专职……我的心在暗中嫉妒他们的道德，作为胜利者，我想与失败者齐身。" 他说他开始厌恶野蛮与杀戮，喜爱文明与仁义。

铁木真心里始终放不下他的初恋情人，于是他命令士兵传来那个女子，易达迷。铁木真乞求易达迷和

business is to destroy... My heart in secret is jealous of their virtues; I would wish, as a conqueror, to imitate the vanquished." He said he began to feel sick of barbarism and slaughtering, and to be fond of civilization, justice and virtues.

Genghis Khan, in his heart, could never forget his first love. Then, he ordered the guard to bring that woman, Idame, to the palace. Genghis Khan begged Idame to divorce her husband and marry him to be the empress. Idame told him that the folk customs and protocols did not allow her to do that. She could not divorce her husband. At this moment, Idame's servant, Asseli, and her husband Zamti all persuaded Idame, and hoped that she could marry Genghis Khan, because this was the easiest way to save the crown prince. But Idame refused.

She proposed that Zamti could, in the name of the crown prince, call on the people to start an armed rebellion to resist and fight against the army of Genghis Kwan.

Act V

The armed rebellion failed. Octar sent under escort Idame to see Genghis Khan. Idame prayed to the heaven in her heart, begging that the heaven could make Genghis Khan civilized, benevolent and moral, just like her husband Zamti.

When Genghis Khan met Idame, he once again begged

丈夫离婚，嫁给他做皇后。易达迷说中原的风俗习惯和礼仪不允许她这么做，她不能和丈夫离婚。这时，易达迷的女仆阿赛利和他的丈夫扎迷惕都劝易达迷，希望她能够嫁给铁木真，这样就可以更容易地拯救皇太子了。易达迷没有答应。

她建议扎迷惕，可以用皇太子的旗号，号召大家发动武装暴动，反抗铁木真的军队。

第五幕

武装暴动失败了。窝阔台押送易达迷去见铁木真。易达迷暗暗向上天祷告，祈求上天能够让铁木真也具有文明和仁德，就如同她的丈夫扎迷惕那样。

铁木真见到易达迷，再一次乞求易达迷和她丈夫离婚，然后嫁给他。他许诺说，如果她嫁给他，他将收养她和扎迷惕的儿子、不杀害她的丈夫和皇太子。易达迷没有立即答应。她要求与她的丈夫扎迷惕见一面。

易达迷和扎迷惕两人被安排在一个小房间内相见。易达迷对丈夫说："我们要自杀，不要等待刽子手杀死我们。"她把准备好的一把短剑交给丈夫，要求丈夫用短剑先结束她的生命。扎迷惕颤抖着不敢那样去做。易达迷非常气愤，抓住她丈夫的手臂喊道：

her to divorce her husband, and then marry him. He promised: if she married him, he would adopt her and Zamti's son, and would not kill her husband and the crown prince. Idame did not agree to his suggestions immediately. She asked to see her husband Zamti again.

Idame and Zamti were arranged to meet in a small room. Idame said to her husband: "Let us die, and don't wait to be slaughtered." She then handed a dagger to her husband and asked her husband to kill her with the dagger. Zamti was shivering and dared not to do that. Idame flied into a rage, and held her husband's arm and shouted: "Kill me!" At this moment, Genghis Khan and his soldiers arrived and seized the dagger from Zamti. Facing the unyielding spirit of the two, the soul of Genghis Khan was shocked and purified. He decided he would no longer kill anybody, nor would he compel Idame to marry him. Furthermore, he decided to appoint Zamti as a moral preacher to teach his ministers and officials

This is the basic plot of *The Orphan of China* by Voltaire.

We could find that *The Orphan of China*, adapted on the basis of *The Orphan of Zhao*, made a lot of changes. In addition to the differences in the names and setup of the characters, there are also tremendous differences in terms of the development and time of the entire story. Ji Junxiang's *The Orphan of Zhao* tells the story from the

蒙古骑兵
Mongolian cavalry.

"杀!"这时,铁木真和他的士兵赶到,铁木真急忙夺下了扎迷惕的短剑。面对二人这种宁死不屈的精神,铁木真的心灵受到了震动与净化。他决定不再屠杀任何人,也不再逼易达迷嫁给她,并且还聘请扎迷惕做他的道德宣讲师,以教育他的大臣。

这就是伏尔泰的《中国孤儿》的大致情节。

我们可以发现,改编后的《中国孤儿》在《赵氏

birth of the orphan to his revenge when he grew up. The time span is about 20 years, and the places frequently change according to the development of the story. For example, the orphan was confined to the mansion by Tu Angu when he was born, the fake orphan of Zhao was killed in Taiping Village, the orphan of Zhao learned his identity when he was in the mansion of Cheng Ying, and the arrest of Tu Angu was made in a bustling market. So the places of the story were changing frequently. In *The Orphan of China* by Voltaire, however, the crown prince was always an infant, it did not tell his growth story, and all events happened on the same day at the same place. Furthermore, *The Orphan of Zhao* tells a pure revenge story characterized by its tense and violent atmosphere, while *The Orphan of China* tells a kind of love story amid the environment of cruel slaughtering.

Perhaps, people would ask this question: *The Orphan of China* by Voltaire and *The Orphan of Zhao* were so different, was he afraid that people would criticize his play and would not accept his *The Orphan of China*? In fact, if we have a better understanding about the concept of drama and the characters of play creation in the times of Voltaire, we would then know and accept it.

In the times of Voltaire, there was a rule to follow and to abide by in play creation—the Three Unities, and the audiences also loved plays created according to the

孤儿》的基础上，有着很多的舍弃。先不说人物的名称与设置上，两者有着很大的差别，就是整体故事的情节发展与故事的发生时间，也都有着很大的不同。纪君祥的《赵氏孤儿》，讲述了赵氏孤儿从初生到成年报仇的故事，这当中的时间跨度是近20年，并且它的故事发生地点也是随着故事的发展而不断地变化。如赵氏孤儿出生时是在被屠岸贾软禁的府中，假赵氏孤儿被杀则是在太平庄上，赵氏孤儿得知身世是在程婴的府邸，而捉拿屠岸贾则是在闹市，可以说，地点是在不断转换的。而在伏尔泰的《中国孤儿》中，皇太子一直是个婴儿，根本没有成长的过程，所发生的事情都是在同一天内的同一个地点。再者，《赵氏孤儿》中紧张而暴力的纯正的仇杀故事，到了《中国孤儿》中，则是在血腥杀戮的气氛中弥漫着浪漫爱情。

也许有的人会问了：伏尔泰的《中国孤儿》和纪君祥的《赵氏孤儿》有着这么大的不同，他不怕别人批评他的剧作、不接受他的《中国孤儿》吗？如果我们了解一下伏尔泰所处时代的戏剧观和戏剧创作特点，我们就会比较容易理解伏尔泰为什么会如此改编了。

requirements of the rule. At that time, plays about heroes were popular on the stage, and some people criticized Voltaire for not being able to create plays about love. Voltaire, who was stubborn, unyielding and talented, would not agree to this criticism for not being able to create plays about love, but at the same time, he was not willing to create any play about love that the audiences did not like. Then, an idea came up to his mind: he would create a play combining the features of the popular plays about heroes with plays about love. With this idea, he created *The Orphan of China* and incorporated the features of the two types into this play. By doing so, Voltaire gave full consideration to the habits of the audiences in watching the plays, and at the same time, he exceeded the expectations of the audiences in appreciating the plays, and the audiences would then not care about how Voltaire adapted his play from *The Orphan of Zhao*. *The Orphan of China* by Voltaire won appreciation and praises from the audiences.

On August 20, 1755, *The Orphan of China* by Voltaire made its official debut, performed by the actors and actresses from Comedie-Francaise (Theatre Francais). It was warmly received by the public and caused a stir in the theater of France and Europe. Later, *The Orphan of China* was also performed in the royal palaces and was highly praised by the royal family members.

The audiences loved the play *The Orphan of China*, and

在伏尔泰的时代，创作戏剧有必须遵守的规律，那就是"三一律"，观众也喜欢按照这样的要求创作出来的戏剧。同时，那时的剧坛流行英雄剧，也有人批评说伏尔泰不会写爱情剧。倔强好胜、才华横溢的伏尔泰当然不会承认自己不能创作爱情剧，同时也不想创作观众不喜欢的爱情剧，于是把流行的英雄剧与爱情剧相结合的创作想法，就在他的头脑中产生了。他把这一切都用在了《中国孤儿》上。这样，伏尔泰既完全考虑到大众的戏剧欣赏习惯，又突破了大众对他的戏剧创作的欣赏期待，自然就不会有观众纠缠于伏尔泰在多大程度上按《赵氏孤儿》剧作进行改编。他的《中国孤儿》赢得了观众的青睐与掌声。

1755年8月20日，伏尔泰的《中国孤儿》正式由法兰西喜剧院的演员在巴黎公演，受到了公众的热烈欢迎，轰动了法国和欧洲的剧坛，盛况空前。此后，《中国孤儿》还在王宫演出，受到了王室的好评。

不仅观众喜欢看，剧评家也乐意对这部剧作些评论，无论是批评还是赞扬。如德拉·摩尔利埃的《对悲剧〈中国孤儿〉的分析》、小普安西奈的《就〈中国孤儿〉问题写给一位老友的书简》、喀宗·杜尔希

the critics were also very willing to write reviews and comments to criticize or praise this play. For example, *Analysis of the Tragedy—The Orphan of China*, *The Letters to a Friend on the Questions about The Orphan of China*, and *Some Comments and Views on The Orphan of China* were all critic reviews on *The Orphan of China*. In February 1756, the *Edinburgh Review* also published an article on *The Orphan of China*, which said: "In his (Voltaire) recent tragedy *The Orphan of China*, he perfectly showed his talent in creation. When we read this work, we, on the one hand, were very delighted, and on the other hand, also had a weird feeling, because he successfully showed both the solemnity of the Chinese ethics and morality and the rudeness of the barbarian Tartar on the French stage. At the same time, the play did not contradict the meticulous rules of the French theatre." From this article, we could see that the author spoke so highly of Voltaire and his play.

When the play *The Orphan of China* was so popular and well received, the publishers also seized the opportunity to publish *The Orphan of China* and printed it again and again. In order to trace to the sources, the Paris publishers also compiled *The Orphan of Zhao, a Chinese Tragedy*, by Ma Yuese, that was published 20 years earlier, as well as the relevant critic reviews, and published them to satisfy the readers' needs.

Of course, amid praises, there were also critical

奈的《对〈中国孤儿〉的看法》等，都是评论《中国孤儿》的文章。在1756年2月的《爱丁堡评论》上，也有一篇评论《中国孤儿》的文章，文中说："在他（伏尔泰）最近的悲剧《中国孤儿》里，他的创作天才尤为突出。我们读了这部作品，一方面觉得高兴，一方面又觉得奇怪，因为他把中国道德的严肃与鞑靼野蛮的粗犷一齐搬上法国舞台，而同时与法国人最讲究的谨严细致的各种规矩毫无抵触之处。"从中我们可以看出，作者对伏尔泰的评价相当高。

《中国孤儿》如此受欢迎，出版商们也及时出版了《中国孤儿》，并且不断再版。为了追根溯源，巴黎出版界还把在20年前发表的马约瑟的《中国悲剧〈赵氏孤儿〉》及相关评论，重新印刷，单册发行，以满足观众的阅读需求。

当然，《中国孤儿》所迎来的不全是赞颂，也有相反的声音。如为《中国孤儿》的诞生起到"巨大推动作用"的卢梭，自然于其中看出伏尔泰对他的反驳，好辩的他肯定不甘沉默。他曾评论《中国孤儿》说："大家从未看到过如此之多的呆头呆脑的傻瓜，舞台上充斥着这类人物，咖啡馆中也回荡着这些人的

voices on *The Orphan of China*. For example, Rousseau, who played a "tremendous driving role" in the birth of *The Orphan of China*, naturally read between the lines and sensed the disapproval of him by Voltaire. He, so argumentative, was not willing to remain silent. He once commented *The Orphan of China* like this: "We have never seen so many idiotic characters on the stage. The quotations and words are echoing in coffee shops, and their works can be seen on the platforms of stations. I heard some people criticize *The Orphan of China*. The public are praising it, but an awkward writer who was unable to see the flaws would manage to feel the beauty from it." British writer Arthur Murphy (1727–1805), after watching *The Orphan of China* by Voltaire, also felt that it was not perfectly written, and got a plan that he would re-adapt *The Orphan of Zhao*, so that he could compete with *The Orphan of China* by Voltaire. Murphy did not stop at the planning stage, and he did adapt his version of *The Orphan of China*.

Due to the position of Voltaire in the French literature circles and the stir *The Orphan of China* caused in France, a craze for Chinese drama swept across Europe, and at the same time, the "China fever" also reached its climax in France and Europe.

格言警句，车站的月台上也充满了他们的著作。我听到了有人批判《中国孤儿》。因为虽然大家都在欢呼它，但对于一位不大能从中看到其瑕疵的蹩脚作家来说，才勉强能感到其中的美。"英国的作家亚瑟·墨菲看到伏尔泰的《中国孤儿》，也感到写得还不够完美，从而令他有了重新改编《赵氏孤儿》的想法，以期与伏尔泰的《中国孤儿》一较高低。墨菲没有停留在想象的阶段，而是真的改编出一部墨氏《中国孤儿》。

由于伏尔泰在法国文坛的地位，和他的《中国孤儿》在法国引起的轰动，整个欧洲掀起了一股中国剧热潮，同时也把法国乃至欧洲流行的"中国热"推向了高潮。

Pantheon Group

At the beginning of the 18th century, Duke Philippe de Vendome of France was an illegitimate son of King Henry IV. He was once a general and later became the abbot of an abbey, but such positions could not satisfy his ambitions for power. With him, there were many disfavored aristocrats and talented litterateurs and artists who were not widely accepted in the society. They worshipped the doctrine of Epicurus to maximize the happiness, and lived a luxurious and lewd life. They, while indulged in drinking and pleasure-seeking, also criticized the government and social problems, and expressed their inner sufferings. People called this small group of people, who were indulged in pleasure-seeking and also criticized the government, the Pantheon Group.

"Three Unities"

The "Three Unities" is the theory on the structure of classical plays in Europe. This was first raised by Italian drama theorists during the Renaissance, and was later confirmed and promoted by French classical dramatists. This rule stipulates that the play creation must follow the unities of time, place and action, that is, a play should have only one story plot, and the story should happen in one day and at one place. French classical drama theorist Nicolas Boileau-Despreaux explained, "Tell a complete story, from the beginning to the ending, happening in one day at one place." After the 18th century, with the emergence of romantic drama, the "Three Unities" rule was constantly criticized by dramatists and was gradually smashed in the practice of drama creation.

圣殿集团

　　18世纪初，法国的菲力浦·德·望笃姆公爵是亨利四世的私生子，他做过将军，后来成为了法兰西大修道院院长，不过这样的职位依然没有满足他的雄心壮志。于是，在他周围，就聚集了很多失意的王公贵族、有才华而没有得到社会认可的文学家、艺术家。他们奉伊壁鸠鲁的享乐主义为信条，过着奢侈、淫荡的生活。他们在觥筹交错、放纵淫荡之余，抨击朝政、针砭时弊，以抒发内心不得志的苦闷。这样的一个既讲究享乐又抨击朝政的小团体，人们称它为"圣殿集团"。

"三一律"

　　"三一律"是欧洲古典主义戏剧结构理论，先由文艺复兴时期意大利戏剧理论家提出，后为法国古典主义戏剧家确定和推行。它规定剧本创作必须遵守时间、地点和行动的一致，即一部剧本只允许写单一的故事情节，戏剧行动必须发生在一天之内和一个地点。法国古典主义戏剧理论家布瓦洛解释为"要用一地、一天内完成的一个故事从开头直到末尾维持着舞台充实"。18世纪以后，随着浪漫主义戏剧的兴起，"三一律"不断受到戏剧家的抨击，逐渐被创作实践突破。

IV

The Appeal of *The Orphan of Zhao* in Europe

The Orphan of Zhao, a Chinese Tragedy translated by Joseph Marie de Premare aroused great response just after it was published in France. It can be said that *The Orphan of China* adapted by Voltaire based on it was representative in the response. But the appeal of *The Orphan of Zhao* was not only limited to this as it was almost popular in the whole Europe. Thanks to Voltaire's *The Orphan of China,* Europe's "China fever" quickly reached the climax. Many dramatists adapted *The Orphan of Zhao* successively and the "enthusiasm for the orphan" prevailed in European theatres.

The first writer who adapted *The Orphan of Zhao* is William Hatchett (c. 1730–1768) of Britain. Hatchett always paid attention to Chinese culture. He was deeply moved by the story when he read this Chinese drama and made up his mind to adapt it. He did so not only because he loved Chinese dramas, but also because he hoped to point out ills of the times. This is probably the main

4

《赵氏孤儿》在欧洲的魅力

马约瑟翻译的《中国悲剧〈赵氏孤儿〉》在法国一面世，就引起了巨大的反响。可以说，伏尔泰据之改编的《中国孤儿》，是这些反响中比较有代表性的。不过，《赵氏孤儿》的魅力，并不仅限于此，它几乎风靡了全欧洲，在伏尔泰《中国孤儿》的推波助澜下，欧洲的"中国热"迅速达到了顶峰，众多戏剧家纷纷对《赵氏孤儿》进行改编，欧洲剧坛"孤儿热"风行。

第一位改编《赵氏孤儿》的作家是英国的威廉·哈切特（约1730—1768）。哈切特一贯关注中国文化，当他看到这部来自中国的戏剧作品时，被它的故事深深打动，决心进行改编。哈切特对《赵氏孤儿》进行改编，并不是仅仅出于对这部来自中国的戏剧的喜欢，而是希望用它的故事来针砭时弊。这可能

reason why he chose to adapt the story.

The prime minister of Britain when Hatchett lived was Robert Walpole (1676–1745). He began to take office from the 1820s and maintained his long-term rule by a bribery system and a spoil-dividing system. He himself was jealous of the capable and appointed the fraudulent. In respect of the British diplomatic policy, he advocated concession without achievements, which led Britain to consecutive failures in the war with Spain. All the British sagacious objected to his corrupt rule and organized an opposition party jointly to struggle against the ruling party represented by him. Both Hatchett and Marshal Agger the Duke were members of the opposition party and their relationship was quite close. Hatchett adapted *The Orphan of Zhao* and dedicated the adapted drama to Agger the Duke as a weapon in the struggle against the ruling party represented by Robert Walpole.

The drama adapted by Hatchett from *The Orphan of Zhao* is also called *The Orphan of China*. It retains the main paragraphs and outlines of *The Orphan of Zhao, a Chinese Tragedy* translated by Ma Yuese, such as searching for the orphan, saving the orphan, eliminating the traitor and repaying the debt of gratitude, and only differs slightly from *The Orphan of Zhao* in two acts. But Hatchett changed the characters considerably; for instance, he changed Tu Angu to Xiao He, Cheng Ying to Kai Feng, Han Jue to Su

罗伯特·沃尔波尔像
A portrait of Robert Walpole.

也是他选择改编《赵氏孤儿》的主要原因。

在哈切特生活时代的英国,当权首相是罗伯特·沃尔波尔(1676—1745)。他从18世纪20年代起,就执掌政权,以贿赂制度、分赃制度维持长期的统治,而且他本人嫉贤妒能、任奸用诈。在英国的外交政策上,主张无为退让,致使与西班牙的战争连连失利。英国的贤人志士都反对罗伯特·沃尔波尔首相的腐朽统治,联合起来组成在野党,与以罗伯特·沃尔波尔首相为代表的执政党进行斗争。哈切特与战功卓著的元帅阿格尔公爵都是在野党成员,二人的关系非常密切。哈切特改编《赵氏孤儿》,并把改编后的剧本献给阿格尔公爵,以之作为与以罗伯特·沃尔波尔首相为代表的执政党进行斗争的武器。

哈切特改编《赵氏孤儿》的剧本也叫做《中国孤儿》,它保留了马约瑟《中国悲剧〈赵氏孤儿〉》的主要段落及轮廓,如搜孤、救孤、除奸、报恩,仅最

Sheng, Gongsun Chujiu to Laozi and the orphan of Zhao to Kang Xi. He also added Lü Bin as the wife of Kai Feng fictitiously. These names apparently do not conform to the Chinese history and we can only regard them as names of characters in the drama. Hatchett adapted the story this way because of his need for political struggle. For example, he imagined Prime Minister Xiao He as British Prime Minister, Robert Walpole and taunted, satirized and attacked him as much as possible. When he described Xiao He in Scene 2, Act 2 of *The Orphan of China*, he said: "When Xiao He was triumphant, China suffered. He was still clever and could defeat enemies in this country. But to the Tatars and Mongolians, he had become a puppet long before.

Hatchett's *The Orphan of China* is also composed of five acts.

Act 1: Kai Feng and Wu Sangui talked about how Prime Minister Xiao He played politics, framed the Great General Europa who had accomplished illustrious military exploits and killed all the more than 300 people in his family. Europa escaped. His son Jinwang Ama was the emperor's son-in-law and his daughter-in-law was pregnant. Guard Commander Su Sheng received Xiao He's order and asked Jinwang Ama to commit suicide. Before the emperor's son-in-law died, he asked the princess to name the orphan Kang Xi after birth to

西洋自鸣钟,采用了中西合璧的艺术手法制成。
Western chime clock, integrates Chinese and Western craft technologies.

后两幕稍与《赵氏孤儿》不同。不过哈切特对于剧中人物的改动比较大,如把屠岸贾改成了萧何、程婴改成了开封、韩厥改成了苏生、公孙杵臼改成了老子、赵氏孤儿改成了康熙,又虚构增添了开封的妻子吕宾,这些名字,显然与中国的历史是不相符合的,我们也只能当作剧本人物名称对待。哈切特如此改编,也完全是出于他政治斗争的需要。如他把首相萧何就

revenge the whole family. Xiao He and the monk knew Orphan Kang Xi was born and planned to kill him. Kai Feng found Princess Ama Wang and promised to save the orphan Kang Xi. After the princess handed over the orphan, she killed herself.

Act 2: Kai Feng held Kang Xi in his arms and went out of the emperor's son-in-law's mansion. He was encountered by Guard Commander Su Sheng at the gate. Kai Feng persuaded him with principles of righteousness and Su Sheng was moved. He let Kai Feng and Kang Xi go and killed himself. After Xiao He heard of this, he flew into a rage and ordered all nationals to hand over male babies under 6 months old within 3 days. In order to save Kang Xi and all male babies in the nation, Kai Feng went to Laozi, a secluded old minister, for a countermeasure. The two finally decided to hand over Kai Feng's male baby under one month old to Laozi to substitute Kang Xi and Kai Feng went to Xiao He to inform against Laozi so as to save Kang Xi and all male babies in the nation.

Act 3: Lü Bin, the wife of Kai Feng, could not harden her heart to sacrifice her son and didn't agree to hand over the baby. The couple argued with each other. Kai Feng talked her over and Lü agreed to hand over her son in the end. Xiao He arrested Laozi and the fake Kang Xi according to Kai Feng's information and both Laozi and the fake Kang Xi were killed.

假想成了英国首相罗伯特·沃尔波尔，在剧中对其极尽嘲讽、挖苦和攻击。在《中国孤儿》的第二幕第二场中写到萧何时说："萧何成功，中国受苦。他依然多巧，能打败本国的敌人，可是对于鞑靼和蒙古人，他早成了傀儡。"

哈切特的《中国孤儿》，也由五幕组成。

第一幕：开封和吴三桂谈论首相萧何如何耍奸弄权，阴谋陷害拥有赫赫战功的大将军欧罗巴，将欧罗巴一家三百多口满门抄斩。欧罗马逃走了。他的儿子金王阿妈是驸马，儿媳阿妈王氏身怀六甲。警卫司令苏生奉萧何的命令要驸马金王阿妈自尽。驸马自尽前，嘱咐公主要给将产下的孤儿取命康熙，为全家报仇。萧何与和尚知道孤儿康熙降生，于是谋划杀害康熙。开封找到公主阿妈王氏，答应救助孤儿康熙。公主交出孤儿后就自尽了。

第二幕：开封抱着康熙走出驸马府，在大门口让警备司令苏生碰上了。开封晓之以大义，令苏生侠气顿生，放走了开封和康熙，并随即自杀身亡。萧何得知此事后，通令全国把六个月以下的男婴统统交出，限时三天。为了救助康熙和全国的小男婴，开封找到

Act 4: Xiao He was ambitious and wanted to kill Emperor Gao of the Han Dynasty of the Jin Kingdom. Kai Feng and his friend Wu Sangui discussed and painted the course how Europa's whole family were killed on a robe to wait for an opportunity to expose Xiao He's plot. Later, the ministers exposed Xiao He to Emperor Gao one after another, but the emperor asked them to take out evidence.

Act 5: The war between China and Tatars broke out. When Xiao He talked about the setbacks in the war with

Chinese screens with Western portraits and street scenery.

退隐的老臣老子商议对策。最后两人决定：开封把自己的不满月的男孩交给老子，假扮康熙，自己去向萧何告发老子，从而使康熙和全国的男婴免受杀戮。

第三幕：开封的妻子吕宾不忍心牺牲自己的孩子，不同意交出自己的孩子，夫妻二人起了争执。在开封的劝说下，吕宾最后同意交出自己的孩子。开封告发后，萧何逮到了老子和假康熙。老子和假康熙一起被杀害。

第四幕：萧何野心勃勃，想谋害晋君汉高帝。开封和他的朋友吴三桂商议，把欧罗巴全家被谋杀的经过画在一件袍子上，等待时机，向汉高帝揭发萧何的阴谋。后来，群臣纷纷向汉高帝揭发首相萧何图谋不轨，不过，汉高帝要求他们要拿出证据来。

第五幕：中国和鞑靼发生战争。当萧何与汉高帝谈论战争失利的时候，开封拿出了那件画有欧罗巴全家受害过程的袍子，控诉了萧何的阴谋与野心，于是萧何伏罪，被拿下正法。汉高帝把萧何的家产全部充公，赏给了曾经救助过康熙的人，并给老子修建了一座庄严肃穆的坟墓。全剧在一片欢呼声中结束。

哈切特的《中国孤儿》是在1741年出版的，要比

Emperor Gao of the Han Dynasty, Kai Feng took out the robe painted with the course how Europa's whole family were killed and denounced Xiao He's plot and conspiracy. Thus Xiao He had to plead guilty and was pushed out and executed. Emperor Gao had Xiao He's property confiscated, gave it to those who had helped Kang Xi and had a grand and solemn tomb built for Laozi. The drama ends in cheers.

Hatchett's *The Orphan of China* was published in 1741, many years earlier than Voltaire's adaptation. But the pity is that Hatchett's play had never been staged for the audience. But there was also something satisfactory: in the second year when the drama was published, i.e. 1742, the Prime Minister Robert Walpole fell from power and the prophecy in *The Orphan of China* was realized.

Murphy, another British writer who adapted *The Orphan of Zhao*, believed Voltaire's adaptation left much to be desired and decided to readapt it to better transmit the story and its chivalrous spirit.

Before Voltaire finished adapting *The Orphan of Zhao*, Murphy had planned to adapt *The Orphan of Zhao, a Chinese Tragedy* translated by Ma Yuese. After he heard that Voltaire was adapting it to a drama, he gave up this idea temporarily and wanted to wait and see whether Voltaire's adaptation was successful. If Voltaire's adaptation was successful, he would not adapt it. He

伏尔泰的《中国孤儿》早很多年。不过，令人遗憾的是，哈切特的《中国孤儿》却没能通过舞台表演与观众见面。当然，也有令人欣慰的事，那就是在剧作出版的第二年，即1742年，剧中所嘲讽的罗伯特·沃尔波尔首相就倒台了。《中国孤儿》的预言实现了。

英国的另一位改编《赵氏孤儿》的作家亚瑟·墨菲则认为伏尔泰的《中国孤儿》还有不尽人意之处，于是他决定重新改编，从而使《赵氏孤儿》的故事与侠义精神更好地传播。

在伏尔泰改编《赵氏孤儿》完成前，墨菲曾计划根据马约瑟翻译的《中国悲剧〈赵氏孤儿〉》进行改编。他听说伏尔泰正在进行此剧的改编后，就暂时放弃了这个念头，想等伏尔泰改编完成后，看一下是否成功，如果伏尔泰的改编比较完美，他就不再改编此剧。等到1756年，墨菲读到了伏尔泰的《中国孤儿》。他认为伏尔泰的《中国孤儿》存在很多缺点。墨菲曾给伏尔泰写过一封公开信，在信里列举了伏尔泰的《中国孤儿》的种种不足，如剧中穿插一段成吉思汗向易达迷求婚的情节，是把粗豪的铁木真变成了谈情说爱、儿女情长的法兰西式的骑士，且中间缺乏

read Voltaire's *The Orphan of China* in 1756 and believed there were many shortcomings in it. He wrote an open letter to Voltaire, listing the shortcomings in his play. For example, the episode of Genghis khan making an offer of marriage to Idame depicted the tough Genghis khan as a French-style amorous knight and the transition and foreshadowing were apparently lacking in between, which made the episode quite abrupt and inharmonious with the theme of the drama. Owing to the insertion of this episode, the plot of the whole drama became loose and less intense. Voltaire's *The Orphan of China* was not only lacking in an intense and heated atmosphere, but also lacking in obvious dramatic plots. What was in the drama was always the baby and this could not push forward development of the plot. It was better to change the orphan to a youth as it was more helpful for depiction of the characters and development of the plot. Hence Murphy started from his own understanding and insight, summarized the information from Voltaire's *The Orphan of China* and *The Orphan of Zhao, a Chinese Tragedy* translated by Ma Yuese and finally finished his adaptation of *The Orphan of China* more than three years later in 1759.

Murphy's *The Orphan of China* is like this: first, he narrated in a way of account that the Genghis Khan invaded the middle of China 20 years ago and killed all Chinese royal families, but a prince survived because

明显的过渡铺垫，显得非常突兀，与全剧的基调不相谐调。由于这个情节的穿插，使得全剧剧情松懈，失去了张力；伏尔泰的《中国孤儿》缺乏紧张激烈的气氛，也缺乏非常明显的戏剧性情节；剧中孤儿始终是婴儿，对剧情的发展起不到推动作用，不如把孤儿换作处于青年时期，这样更能有助于人物刻画和情节发展。于是，墨菲从自己独到的理解与识见出发，综合伏尔泰的《中国孤儿》和马约瑟翻译的《中国悲剧〈赵氏孤儿〉》所提供的信息，历经三年多，终于在1759年完成了自己的改编本——《中国孤儿》。

墨菲的《中国孤儿》的故事是这样的：首先，用交待的方式述说20年前，铁木真入侵中原大地，杀尽了中国的皇室家族，但有一个皇子却因是遗腹子而幸存下来。为拯救这位皇子，大臣扎迷惕将自己的儿子假作皇子，悄悄送往高丽，将皇子假作自己的亲生儿子，留在身边精心抚养。20年后，成吉思汗再

墨菲的英文版《中国孤儿》扉页
The head page of The Orphan of Zhao, a Chinese Tragedy adapted by Murphy.

he was a posthumous child. In order to save the prince, Minister Zamti disguised his son as the prince and sent him to Korea secretly, while disguised the prince as his own son and fostered him carefully in his home. Twenty years later, Genghis khan occupied the city of Beijing again and Zamti's son in Korea went back to resist Genghis khan and defend the nation. Unfortunately, he was captured by Genghis Khan's troop. Genghis Khan doubted this 20-years-old youth was the prince who he hadn't killed 20 years before but could not confirm it. Hence Genghis khan fetched Zamti, forced him to say the whereabouts of the princes and threatened: "If you don't say the whereabouts of the prince, I will kill all the 20-years-old youths in the nation." Out of his loyalty to the late emperor and his love for the people, Zamti told a lie that the arrested youth was the prince and decided to sacrifice his own son to save the prince and all the youths in the whole nation. Zamti told the truth to the prince and his own son and Zamti's wife also learned of the truth. Out of maternal love, she could not bear to let her own son die. When she was interrogated, she told some of the truth intermittently. Genghis Khan flew into a shameful rage and tortured the couple cruelly to extort a confession. At the critical moment, a bosom friend of Zamti, in spite of all the dangers, maneuvered most of Genghis Khan's troops out of Beijing with a plot and pretended to claim

次攻占北京城。这时，在高丽的扎迷惕的儿子，赶回来抵抗成吉思汗，参加保家卫国的战争。不幸的是，他被铁木真的军队俘虏了。铁木真怀疑这位20岁的年轻人，就是他在20年前没有杀死的皇子，但他又不能确认。于是，成吉思汗就找来扎迷惕，逼问他皇子的下落，并威胁说：如果不讲出皇子的下落，就杀死全国所有20岁的青年人。扎迷惕出于对先王的忠诚和对人民的仁爱，谎说那个被逮捕的青年就是皇子，决定牺牲亲生儿子来挽救皇子和全国的青年。扎迷惕将真情告诉了皇子和自己的儿子。扎迷惕的妻子也知道了真相，不忍心让自己的儿子受死，在被审问时，断断续续中讲出了部分实情。铁木真恼羞成怒，对扎迷惕夫妇严刑逼供。扎迷惕的挚友在此紧急关头，不顾危险，用计谋将铁木真的大部分军队调离北京城，并谎称皇子已经在战乱中被杀死。铁木真当然不相信他的话，就命他提来皇子的头，以证明皇子真的已死。这时，身藏利器的真皇子被带到铁木真面前，二人一照面便兵刃相见。经过一番恶战，铁木真被皇子杀死，报了20年前的冤仇。扎迷惕由于受刑过重，生命垂危，在向皇子留下遗嘱后，便咽下了最后一口气。他

that the prince had been killed in the war. Genghis Khan certainly didn't believe what he said and ordered him to prove the prince's death by his head. At the moment, the true prince hiding a sharp sword was brought in front of Genghis Khan and the two fought against each other. After a fierce fight, Genghis Khan was killed by the prince in revenge of the hatred 20 years ago. Because of the cruel torture, Zamti breathed his last after leaving the prince a will. Zamti's wife could not stand the agony of losing her husband, and she killed herself by a sword out of deep self-condemnation.

After Murphy finished *The Orphan of China* in 1795, it was staged publicly in the Drewry Blue Theater in London in April that year. Unexpectedly, his play also achieved great success as Voltaire's. It was staged nine times in a row and was warmly welcomed by the audience. Newspapers also published specials to review his drama. An article read when describing the stage effect: "We saw that many gardens were arranged in an oriental style, the front of many houses were decorated with curved lines and many rooms were fraught with Chinese vases and Indian pagodas." Such attention to the stage effect is related to the fact that Chinese dramas were seldom staged in Britain. In order to present *The Orphan of China*, the Drewry Blue Theater prepared costly Chinese settings and proper Chinese costumes in particular and used a

的妻子经受不住失去丈夫的痛苦和深深的自责，自刎而死。

墨菲在1759年完成《中国孤儿》后，4月份在伦敦的德鲁里兰剧院进行公演。令人没有想到的是，他的这部《中国孤儿》，和伏尔泰的《中国孤儿》一样，也取得了巨大的成功，连续上演九场，得到了观众的热烈欢迎。报刊也发表专文，对他的剧作进行评论。文章描述当时舞台效果时称："我们看到许多花园被安排成东方的式样，许多房屋的门面点缀着曲折的线条，许多屋子里塞满了中国的花瓶和印度的宝塔。"这种对舞台效果的重视，与英国较少有中国戏剧上演有关。德鲁里兰剧院为了上演《中国孤儿》，还特别制作了名贵的中国布景、合适的中国服装，并且在舞台上大量运用中国色素。舞台综合运用的这些中国元素，是英国观众平时很少能欣赏到的。这无疑也是墨菲的《中国孤儿》演出获得成功的重要因素之一。

墨菲《中国孤儿》的成功，也是因为这样的孤儿故事，契合当时英国国情的需要。当时的英国，在对外战争中，连连吃紧，法国对英国步步紧逼，并且企图通过联合西班牙，进攻英国本土。虽然面临这么糟

lot of Chinese elements on the stage. Comprehensive use of these Chinese elements was rarely seen by the British audience. This doubtlessly conduced to the success of Murphy's *The Orphan of China*.

Murphy's *The Orphan of China* made a success because the story about an orphan coincided with the national situation of Britain at that time. Britain was engaged in an external war and the situation was critical time and again. France pressed on Britain step by step and tried to invade Britain jointly with Spain. Although faced with such a bad diplomatic and military situation, the cabinet composed of political giants still disputed over trifles, undermined one another and did not give priority to the national affairs. King George II was too old to control the political situation while his successor George III was only an orphan in his 20s and those political giants simply didn't think much of this young and inexperienced king. All British people were anxious about such a political situation and hoped George III could make vigorous efforts to turn the tide and assume the heavy responsibility. The young George III also wanted to do something to change the difficult situation in Britain. Murphy's *The Orphan of China* was published at such a time when the whole nation wanted the king's successor, Orphan George III, to accomplish the heroic exploits depicted in the play. A story of an imperial orphan fighting heroically for his family and nation

伏尔泰与《中国孤儿》

乔治三世像
A portrait of King George III.

糕的外交、战争局面，各个政治巨头组成的内阁，还是互相扯皮和拆台，不以国事为重。国王乔治二世已是风烛残年，无法控制政治局面。而继任者乔治三世却是一位20多岁的孤儿，政治巨头根本没有把这位乳臭未干的国王放在眼里，英国的民众都为这样的政治局面而感到痛心疾首，希望乔治三世能够力挽狂澜、担当重任。

年轻的乔治三世也想能够有一番作为，改变英国的困窘局面。就在这样一个全国都希望国王继任者、孤儿乔治三世有英勇行为的背景下，墨菲的《中国孤儿》诞生了，而且描绘的就是皇室遗孤为国难家仇英勇斗争的故事，这无疑迎合了英国民众心理，让他们从这个《中国孤儿》的故事中，看到了英国的希望。就这样，墨菲的《中国孤儿》中新鲜的中国元素结合英国民众的爱国心，使它备受英国观众欢迎，墨菲也被冠以"爱国主义大师"的称号。

doubtlessly conformed to the thinking of British people and rekindled their hope. Thus the fresh Chinese elements in Murphy's *The Orphan of China* combined with British people's patriotism made it warmly welcomed by the British audience and Murphy was also called a "patriotic master."

Murphy's *The Orphan of China* not only achieved great success in Britain but was also spread overseas. It was staged in the South Theatre in Philadelphia, USA, in 1777 and was presented in a theatre on the John Street of New York, USA, in 1778, both successfully.

The British adapted *The Orphan of Zhao* twice, and both for political reasons. The adaptors discovered unlimited appeal in *The Orphan of Zhao* and they placed their earnest expectations on the story.

Apart from France and Britain, some other European writers also adapted *The Orphan of Zhao*.

For example, in Italy, P. Pietro Metastasio (1698–1782) adapted *The Orphan of Zhao, a Chinese Tragedy* translated by Ma Yuese to *The Chinese Hero*.

However, P. Pietro Metastasio's adaptation of *The Orphan of Zhao* was not out of the need for enlightenment like Voltaire, Hatchett or Murphy. In fact, he had received the Austrian empress's order and had to adapt it according to her regulation, which was quite stern as it required that the number of cast should not exceed five

墨菲的《中国孤儿》不仅在英国取得了巨大成功，而且也远播海外。1777年，墨菲的《中国孤儿》在美国费城的南方剧场上演；1778年，在美国纽约约翰大街的剧场上演，都受到了观众的喜爱。

英国人两次改编《赵氏孤儿》，都有着某种政治的意义，改编者看到了《赵氏孤儿》的无穷魅力，他们在《赵氏孤儿》的故事中寄托着自身的强烈愿望。

在法国和英国之外，还有其他一些欧洲国家的作家，也对《赵氏孤儿》进行了改编。

如在意大利，彼得罗·梅塔斯塔齐奥（1698—1782）将马约瑟翻译的《中国悲剧〈赵氏孤儿〉》改编为《中国英雄》。

不过，彼得罗·梅塔斯塔齐奥改编《赵氏孤儿》，不像伏尔泰出于启蒙的需要，也不像哈切特、墨菲出于政治的考量，他接到奥地利皇后的懿旨，必须按照皇后的规定进行改编。皇后的规定是相当苛刻的，要求全剧不能超过五名演员，演出时间不能比规定的长，也不能有任何残忍的情景和令人不愉快的情节。好在彼得罗·梅塔斯塔齐奥有一手，他把全剧压缩成三幕，而且剧中人正好是五位：朗格、席文诺、

in the whole drama, the performance time should not be longer than the prescribed period, and that there should not be any cruel scenes and unpleasant plots. Fortunately, P. Pietro Metastasio was skilful. He condensed the whole drama into three acts and there were only five characters: Lang Ge, Xi Wennuo, Li Xinjia, Urania and Ming Teao.

Because he was limited by too many requirements and the empress did not want to see anything violent and unpleasant, P. Pietro Metastasio could not retain the revenge theme and had to change the originally revengeful drama to a comedy with a happy ending in order to entertain the imperial family.

P. Pietro Metastasio was aware that the adaptation was far from the original drama, and thus the elements of the original play and Chinese culture were not left much. But he still tried to set the play in Chinese settings. For example, he arranged the scene of the story in Xi'an, Shaanxi Province and said in the setting explanation in Scene 1, Act 1: "In the rooms for imprisoning Tartar criminals in the imperial palace, there are some exotic paintings, transparent vessels and colorful carpets. In a word, they are all about the Chinese luxuriousness and exquisiteness." The setting in Scene 7 was: "The imperial palace is magnificent, showing the talent and culture of Chinese people. People can tell the difference between monks, officers and scholars." In these settings, P. Pietro

李辛佳、乌拉尼娅和明特奥。

由于过多的条件限制和皇后不想看到暴力与不愉快的事,彼得罗·梅塔斯塔齐奥无法保留《赵氏孤儿》的报仇主题,不得已把原本的复仇剧,改编成了供宫廷娱乐的大团圆喜剧。

彼得罗·梅塔斯塔齐奥知道如此改编,偏离原剧太远,以至于找不到太多《赵氏孤儿》的影子和中国文化元素。但他还是极力地把剧情设置在中国背景中,如把故事的发生地设置在陕西省西安。在第一幕第一场的布景说明中说:"在皇宫中用于囚禁鞑靼罪犯的房间里,大家于其中发现了一些奇怪的绘画、透明的器皿和色泽鲜艳的地毯。总而言之,是中国人豪华和讲究的一切。"第七场的布景设置是:"皇家大殿内,富丽堂皇,其中表现了中华民族的才能与文化。大家可以于其中区别出僧侣、军官和儒生。"在这些布景设计中,彼得罗·梅塔斯塔齐奥几乎涉及了瓷器、和尚、文人和宝塔等中国元素,他和众多欧洲人一样,认为这些所代表的就是中国。但他的这些中国元素的运用,并没有真正体现出中国味道,相反的却是一种意大利加奥地利的情调,使得整个剧作看起

Metastasio used such Chinese elements as porcelains, monks, men of letters and pagodas. Like many Europeans, he thought that these represented China. However, such Chinese elements did not reflect the real Chinese style and instead, it turned out to be a fusion of the Italian and Austrian styles, which made the whole drama look like a farce.

The main plot of P. Pietro Metastasio's *The Chinese Hero* is like this: Urania and Li Xinjia were sisters and a couple of Tatar princesses. Once they debuted, they received a letter from their father, which said the Tatars became reconciled with the Hans and Li Xinjia could marry the successor to the throne. But Li Xinjia already had her lover Xi Wennuo and Urania also had her beloved Ming Teao. Li Xinjia thought she had to marry that successor and Xi Wennuo was in great distress. Lang Ge, Xi Wennuo's father, remained indifferent to many ministers' hope that he came to the throne and claimed to announce who was the late emperor's orphan on that day. Xi Wennuo was much grieved and thought he would lose Li Xinjia inevitably. Lang Ge told Xi Wennuo he was the orphan of the late emperor and both Xi Wennuo and Li Xinjia were extremely happy. Lang Ge told the story how he sacrificed his son to protect the late emperor's orphan Xi Wennuo. Ming Teao suddenly knelt at the feet of Lang Ge and said he was Lang Ge's son and he didn't die because Al Fenge

来犹如滑稽剧一般。

彼得罗·梅塔斯塔齐奥的《中国英雄》主要剧情是这样的：乌拉尼娅和李辛佳是姐妹，一对鞑靼公主。她们俩一出场，就收到父亲的信，信中说鞑靼与汉人合解了，李辛佳可以嫁给皇位继承人。不过李辛佳已有了自己的情人席文诺，乌拉尼娅也有自己的心上人明特奥。李辛佳以为自己要另嫁给皇位继承人，席文诺心中非常痛苦。席文诺的父亲朗格，面对众多大臣要求他出任国王无动于衷，并声称要在今天宣布谁是先帝的遗孤。席文诺很伤心，认为他必定要失去李辛佳。朗格对席文诺说他就是先帝遗孤，席文诺和李辛佳得知真相，都高兴极了。朗格讲述了他如何牺牲自己的孩子保护先帝遗孤席文诺的事。明特奥突然跪在朗格脚下，说他就是朗格的儿子，他没有死，被阿尔丰格搭救了。朗格喜出望外，李辛佳和席文诺、乌拉尼娅和明特奥双双结成夫妻。

通过戏剧情节的简单介绍，我们可以看出：彼得罗·梅塔斯塔齐奥的《中国英雄》只是保留了《赵氏孤儿》的部分影子，如席文诺是遗孤，朗格为保护遗孤而牺牲自己的孩子。除此之外，这部戏剧已经完全

saved him. Lang Ge was overjoyed. In the end, Li Xinjia married Xi Wennuo and Urania married Ming Teao.

Through the simple introduction of the plot, we can see Pietro Metastasio's *The Chinese Hero* only retained some elements of *The Orphan of Zhao*. For example, Xi Wennuo was an orphan and Lang Ge sacrificed his son to protect the orphan. Except these, this drama is entirely different from *The Orphan of Zhao*, especially that it is strongly amorous. Although the drama was adapted according to the palatial needs, it still tried to keep and promote Chinese culture to the greatest extent, so the imperial family could get to know about the Chinese culture and the role of the "orphan" impressed the European palace.

Besides, we can see from the example of Pietro Metastasio that such an adaptation is no longer a simple dramatic adaptation. Some writers were so infatuated with the story of *The Orphan of Zhao* that they wanted to create a drama about an "orphan" as well.

The great German writer Johann Wolfgang von Goethe (1749–1832, the most important dramatist, poet and thinker of Germany and Europe from the mid-18th century to the beginning of the 19th century) read *The Orphan of Zhao, a Chinese Tragedy* translated by Ma Yuese and was very interested in it. He also wanted to adapt it to a new Chinese drama—*Elpenor*. But Goethe did not finish the drama for an unknown reason and only

伏尔泰与《中国孤儿》

不同于《赵氏孤儿》了，特别是其浓郁的爱情气息。不过，这样一部应宫廷之需求的剧作，还是尽力地保留与宣扬了中国文化，让宫廷窥知了中国文化的一角，让"孤儿"在欧洲的皇宫中留下了自己的身影。

另外我们还可以通过彼得罗·梅塔斯塔齐奥的例子看出，其实这样的改编，不再是纯粹的戏剧改编，而是这些作家心醉于《赵氏孤儿》的故事，他们也要创作"孤儿"剧。

德国大文豪歌德（1749—1832，是18世纪中叶到19世纪初德国和欧洲最重要的剧作家、诗人和思想家）读了马约瑟翻译的《中国悲剧〈赵氏孤儿〉》，对《赵氏孤儿》的故事同样非常感兴趣，也想将其改编成一部新的中国戏剧——《哀兰伯诺》。不过，不知什么原因，歌德并没有完成此剧，仅写出了前两幕。他把完成的部分寄给自己的挚友席勒（1759—1805，德国18世纪著名诗人、哲学家、历史学家和剧作

歌德像
A portrait of Goethe.

149

wrote the first two acts. He sent what he had finished to his bosom friend Johann Christoph Friedrich von Schiller (1759–1805, a famous German poet, philosopher, historian and dramatist in the 18th century and one of the representatives of the German enlightenment literature) to solicit his opinions. Schiller thought highly of it and said this part of the drama was a good work which helped people to look into a writer's mind through his works. In his unfinished adaptation, Goethe arranged such major characters as Li Gu, Elpenor... Therein Elpenor is like the orphan of Zhao in Ji Junxiang's drama. The plot in this part is when Elpenor was a baby, his father was murdered by Li Gu who wanted to usurp the power. Later, Elpenor was brought up by Li Gu as his own son mistakenly. The arrangement of such a plot is apparently similar to that of *The Orphan of Zhao*.

Besides Goethe's *Elpenor*, there is a drama adapted from *The Orphan of Zhao* in Germany. This drama was published anonymously and the name of the drama is *The Chinese or Fare Fate*. It was published in 1774. *The Chinese or Fare Fate* was written in the traditional five acts and in the 6-step iambic verses. Act 1: Minister Han Tong wanted to discriminate against Lan Fu who was his colleague. However, the emperor issued an imperial order at this time and asked Han Tong to marry his daughter Li Lifa to Minister Lan Fu. This made Han Tong angry. Han Tong

德国魏玛国立剧院前的歌德和席勒雕像
The statues of Goethe and Schiller in front of the German National Theatre Weimar.

家，德国启蒙文学的代表人物之一），征求他的意见，席勒对它评价很高，说这部分剧作是引导人们通过作品来窥探作家心灵的好作品。在这部没有完成的改编本中，歌德设置了这样几个主要人物：安提俄普、李古、哀兰伯诺、埃瓦德纳和波利梅蒂斯，其中哀兰伯诺就相当于纪君祥剧作中的赵氏孤儿。这部分的剧情大致是：当哀兰伯诺还是个婴儿时，他的父亲被妄图篡权的李古谋害；而后来哀兰伯诺，却被李古错当作自己的亲生子抚养成人。这种故事情节的设置，显然与《赵氏孤儿》相似。

had an adopted son Kanbul and he and Li Lifa had fallen in love with each other and were engaged privately. Then Han Tong asked Kanbul to kill Lan Fu and promised to marry Li Lifa to him afterwards. Act 2: Kanbul framed Lan Fu and Lan Fu went to Han Tong's mansion for reconciliation, but he was refused stubbornly by Han Tong. Lan Fu felt it was hopeless to become reconciled with Han Tong and went back home and prepared to hit back. Act 3: The emperor believed the treacherous words and wanted to order Lan Fu to commit suicide. Act 4: Lan Fu's father Su Lun told him his true background: he was the orphan Han Tong wanted to track and kill. Su Lun disguised his own son as Lan Fu and his own son had already been killed by Han Tong. Act 5: Han Tong went back on his word to marry Li Lifa to Kanbul and Kanbul killed Han Tong in anger.

Why should the writer want to adapt *The Orphan of Zhao*? The writer himself gave an explanation. He said he wanted to show Chinese characteristics and the "oriental absolutist customs." From this we can also see that introduction of *The Orphan of Zhao* aroused the Germans' strong interest in Chinese culture and they hoped to have a better understanding of China through the adaptation and presentation of this drama.

Fuertaile of Poland also adapted *The Orphan of Zhao, a Chinese Tragedy* translated by Ma Yuese. He also entitled it

除了歌德的《哀兰伯诺》外，德国还有一部改编《赵氏孤儿》的剧作。这部剧作是以匿名的方式发表的，剧名为《中国人或公正的命运》，发表的时间是1774年。《中国人或公正的命运》采取传统戏剧的五幕形式，使用六步抑扬格诗句写成。第一幕：大臣韩同想排斥一起做官的兰福。正在这时，皇帝却降下圣旨，让韩同把女儿莉莉发嫁给大臣兰福，这使韩同甚为恼火。韩同原有一养子坎布尔，坎布尔早已经与莉莉发情投意合、私订终身。韩同就要求坎布尔去除掉兰福，并允诺事成后，就将莉莉发嫁给他。第二幕：坎布尔诬陷兰福，兰福亲自到韩同府上求和，但韩同无论如何不答应和解。兰福感到和解没有希望，回家后就准备进行反击。第三幕：皇帝听信了奸邪之言，欲赐兰福自尽。第四幕：兰福的父亲苏伦告诉了他的真实身世：他就是韩同要追杀的孤儿。苏伦用亲生儿子假作兰福，已被韩同杀死。第五幕：韩同违背了将莉莉发嫁给坎布尔的诺言，坎布尔一怒之下，杀死韩同。

作者为什么要改编《赵氏孤儿》呢？这一点，作者本人曾有所表白，他说是要展现中国的特点和"东

The Orphan of China and had it performed by actors, which won admirations from the audience.

Besides adapting it to dramas, some European writers adapted *The Orphan of Zhao* to novels as well, such as the Russian writer Weilander. He adapted *The Orphan of Zhao* to a Russian novel in 1781 and became the first Russian writer who adapted *The Orphan of Zhao* and the first European writer who adapted it to a novel.

The Orphan of Zhao was translated into French and introduced to Europe by Ma Yuese. It swept across Europe and produced a tremendous influence. After adaptation, the original story of *The Orphan of Zhao* was more or less changed. Hence, in order to present the original story of *The Orphan of Zhao*, writers in some European countries also learnt from Ma Yuese and translated *The Orphan of Zhao* into their own languages successively to let it prevail in their own countries.

In respect of translation of *The Orphan of Zhao*, Britain is just next to Ma Yuese of France. After *Description of the Empire of China and Chinese-Tartary, Together with the Kingdoms of Korea and Tibet; Containing the Geography and History (Natural as well as Civil) of Those Countries* written by Father Du Halde was published, two translations were published in Britain. The first was entitled *Chinese History*, translated by Richard Brook and published by John Watt's publishing house in 1736; the second was translated by

方专制主义的习俗"。我们从中也可以看出,《赵氏孤儿》的传入,让德国人对中国和中国的文化产生了浓厚兴趣,他们想借助这部剧作的改编和上演,对中国有更多的了解。

波兰福尔泰勒也根据马约瑟翻译的《中国悲剧〈赵氏孤儿〉》进行了改编,他的改编剧作也名为《中国孤儿》,并曾让演员演出过,得到了观众的赞赏。

在欧洲,除了把中国的戏剧《赵氏孤儿》改编为戏剧外,还有改编为小说的,如俄国作家魏兰德。他在1781年,把《赵氏孤儿》改编为俄文小说,成为第一位改编《赵氏孤儿》的俄国作家,也是第一位把《赵氏孤儿》改编为小说的欧洲作家。

《赵氏孤儿》是被马约瑟翻译成法文带到欧洲的。它在欧洲的大肆盛行,也不仅仅是停留在被改编上。经过改编,《赵氏孤儿》的原貌或多或少地都被改变了。于是,一些欧洲的国家为了让《赵氏孤儿》以本来面目见人,他们也学起了马约瑟,纷纷把《赵氏孤儿》翻译成本国文字,以便于它在本国流行。

在杜赫德的《中华帝国全志》一书出版后,英国

Edward Caves and published in *Mr. Modern* in 1741. With these English translation, *The Orphan of Zhao, a Chinese Tragedy* had two English versions and was spread across Britain.

By 1762, a third translation of *The Orphan of Zhao* was published in Britain. It was rendered by the sinologist and Dromore Bishop Thomas Percy (1729–1811)and was included in the book *Collection of Chinese Poetry and Prose* compiled by him. Thomas Percy thought that all the previous English versions of *The Orphan of Zhao* had some defects and he said when commenting on the previous English versions and his own translation: "We have no intention of depreciating their value and hereby only declare we have tried our best to retain the features of the original Chinese work carefully and accurately while it had been often regarded as an unnecessary practice in previous translations." Certainly what Thomas Percy said does not mean he translated from the Chinese version of *The Orphan of Zhao*. Instead he still translated from *The Orphan of Zhao, a Chinese Tragedy* which was rendered by Ma Yuese into French and published in *Description of the Empire of China and Chinese-Tartary, Together with the Kingdoms of Korea and Tibet; Containing the Geography and History (Natural as well as Civil) of Those Countries*.

As to whether Ma Yuese had retained the features of the original Chinese work when he translated, Thomas

就出现了两次翻译。第一次是在1736年，理查德·布鲁克翻译的，名叫《中国通史》，由约翰·瓦特的书局出版；第二次是在1741年，爱德华·卡夫斯进行翻译的，载于《绅士杂志》上。这样，伴随着《中华帝国全志》一书的英译，《中国悲剧〈赵氏孤儿〉》就有了两个英文版，并得以在英国传播。

到1762年，英国又有了《赵氏孤儿》的第三个翻译本，它是由汉学家德罗莫尔主教托马斯·帕西（1729—1811）翻译的，收入帕西编著的《中国诗文杂著》一书。托马斯·帕西认为原来的英译本《赵氏孤儿》都存在一些问题，他在评说以前的英译本和自己的翻译时说："我们无意去贬低它们的价值，我们谨于此申明我们尽力仔细和准确地保留了汉文原著的特色，而这些在以往的翻译著作中经常被认为是没有必要的多余做法。"当然，托马斯·帕西如此说，并不是表明他是根据中文版本的《赵氏孤儿》进行翻译的，他翻译所利用的版本，依然是马约瑟翻译成法文的、刊载于《中华帝国全志》上的《中国悲剧〈赵氏孤儿〉》。至于马约瑟翻译时是否准确地保留了汉文原著的特色，他并没有进行考察。在此可以看出，英

Percy did not conduct investigations. It can be seen that there were not only two dramas adapted from *The Orphan of Zhao* but also three English translations of *The Orphan of Zhao* in Britain. Why should Britain have so many versions in such a short period? This indicates that this story was very popular among the British readers.

In 1747, *Description of the Empire of China and Chinese-Tartary, Together with the Kingdoms of Korea and Tibet; Containing the Geography and History (Natural as well as Civil) of Those Countries* by Du Halde was translated into German and therefore *The Orphan of Zhao, a Chinese Tragedy* had the first German version. Later it was put into Russian and the Russian version was developed and published. In 1759, the famous Russian dramatist Sumarokov (1717–1777) translated the play into Russian from its German version by the pen name of M·S and entitled it *The Chinese Tragedy—An Orphan's Monologue*, which was published in the September issue of Diligent Bees in 1759. But what Sumarokov translated into Russian is only a small part of *The Orphan of Zhao*. The lines in Scene 2, Act 1 is just the princess's recitation before she cut her own throat by a sword, as she recalled the dialogue between her and her husband when they bid last farewell to each other. Moreover, the dramatic style of *The Orphan of Zhao* was not retained but concise and lively verse was used in translation. Although the translation does not

国不仅有两部改编《赵氏孤儿》的剧作，还有三个英译本《赵氏孤儿》。为什么在短短的时间内，英国会有这么多的《赵氏孤儿》版本？很显然，这说明《赵氏孤儿》的故事在英国很有市场。

在1747年，杜赫德的《中华帝国全志》被译成德文，这样《中国悲剧〈赵氏孤儿〉》也就有了第一个德文译本。德文版的《中国悲剧〈赵氏孤儿〉》又转译成了俄国文字，形成了在俄国公开发行的俄文版《中国悲剧〈赵氏孤儿〉》。1759年，俄国著名剧作家苏玛罗科夫（1717—1777）依据德文版的《中国悲剧〈赵氏孤儿〉》，以M·S的笔名将其翻译成了俄国文字，译名为《中国悲剧〈孤儿〉的独白》，刊载于《勤劳蜜蜂》杂志1759年的9月号。不过，苏玛罗科夫翻译成俄文的仅仅是《赵氏孤儿》的一小部分：第一幕第二场的台词，也就是剧中公主自刎前追述她的丈夫与其诀别时的一段台词。翻译时也没有保留《赵氏孤儿》的戏剧体裁，而是采用了简洁明快的诗体，在形式上已没有了元杂剧的味道，但是剧情基本上翻译出来了。

在1774年，法文版的《中华帝国全志》被翻译成

have the flavor of a poetic drama of the Yuan Dynasty, the plot was basically rendered.

In 1774, the French edition of *Description of the Empire of China and Chinese-Tartary, Together with the Kingdoms of Korea and Tibet; Containing the Geography and History (Natural as well as Civil) of Those Countries* was translated into Russian. Then, Russia also had a complete Russian version of *The Orphan of Zhao* and the story introduced to Europe by Ma Yuese began to circulate in full in Russia. *The Orphan of Zhao* was not only translated into Russia but a Russian dramatist, Nechayev, also translated Voltaire's adaptation *The Orphan of China* into Russian in 1778 and had it presented publicly in Russia.

The fact that *The Orphan of Zhao* was widely welcomed in Europe is also reflected in the large number of reviews about it.

For example, Marquis Argens, who was influential in France, criticized that there were some defects in the drama of *The Orphan of Zhao* from the classical dramatic view popular in Europe at that time. He said that the writing of *The Orphan of Zhao* didn't follow the "Three Unities" as there were inconsistencies in both the time and scenes of the drama, and that the bloody and cruel scenes were improper and too intense to be staged.

He listed some bloody scenes in the play: Zhao Shuo's wife hanged herself in order to let Cheng Ying rescue

俄文，到此时，俄国也有了俄文版《赵氏孤儿》的全译本，马约瑟带到欧洲的《赵氏孤儿》开始以全貌在俄国流传。俄国不仅翻译了《赵氏孤儿》，1778年，俄国戏剧家涅恰耶夫把伏尔泰改编的《中国孤儿》也翻译成了俄文，并在俄国公开上演，使伏尔泰的《中国孤儿》开始在俄国宫廷和贵族上流社会中广泛流传。

《赵氏孤儿》在欧洲受到广泛的欢迎，还表现在对它大量的评论上。

如在法国比较有影响的阿尔央斯侯爵，他从当时欧洲比较流行的古典主义的戏剧观出发，批评《赵氏孤儿》剧作本身还存在着一些缺陷。阿尔央斯侯爵批评《赵氏孤儿》在写作上没有完全遵循"三一律"，剧中的时间和地点都存在着变化；描述了比较血腥而残忍的场面，这些场面的描述是不得体的，太过于激烈，不能在舞台上表演。

他列举了剧中赵朔妻子刚生下赵氏孤儿后，为了让程婴放心营救赵氏孤儿而上吊自尽，同时还有公孙杵臼被施以棍刑后撞阶身亡、屠岸贾被施以酷刑等这些血腥的场面不应呈现于舞台，而只须作为背景介

the orphan right after she gave birth to the orphan of Zhao; Gongsun Chujiu bumped himself to death against the stair after being clubbed; and Tu Angu was tortured savagely. Marquis Argens pointed out that such scenes should only be briefed and explained to the audience as a background instead of being presented on stage.

Different from Marquis Argens, the English critic Herder praised the drama of *The Orphan of Zhao* and compared it to the ancient Greek tragedies, believing it had reached their artistic height and was a very excellent drama as they were. He also said *The Orphan of Zhao* and ancient Greek tragedies were both successful works in imitation of nature and were similar or identical in the way of writing.

After *The Orphan of Zhao* was introduced to Europe by Ma Yuese, it was favored by Europeans, translated into different languages, commented upon by Europeans constantly and adapted to orphan stories according to the adapters' own norms repeatedly. As a result, such translations, reviews and adaptations aroused strong enthusiasm for *The Orphan of Zhao* in Europe in the mid-18th century and also pushed the "China fever" that emerged at the end of the 17th century in Europe to a climax step by step.

The appeal of *The Orphan of Zhao* gave rise to a trend of selecting Chinese themes in literary creation in Europe.

绍，交待给观众就行了。

与阿尔央斯侯爵不同，英国批评家赫尔德则赞扬《赵氏孤儿》剧作，他把《赵氏孤儿》与古希腊悲剧相比较，认为《赵氏孤儿》达到了古希腊悲剧的艺术高度，是与古希腊悲剧相似的非常优秀的戏剧。他还说，《赵氏孤儿》和古希腊悲剧一样，都是模仿自然的成功作品，在写作方法方面有着相似或一致之处。

马约瑟把《赵氏孤儿》带到欧洲，受到了欧洲人的青睐，不断地被翻译成各国的文字，不断地被欧洲人评头论足，不断地被改编成符合作者自己标准的孤儿故事。这样，经过翻译、评论和改编，使欧洲在18世纪中期风行起了强大的"赵氏孤儿"热，也把在欧洲17世纪末兴起的"中国热"逐步推向了顶峰。

《赵氏孤儿》的魅力，使欧洲在文学创作上兴起了选用中国题材的潮流。如曾经在舞台上演出过的戏剧就有《返回祖国的中国人》、《彬彬有礼的中国人》、《中国人》、《中国饶舌妇》、《阿勒甘在中国》等，都是以中国为故事的背景，表现中国元素。

《赵氏孤儿》在欧洲的影响不仅仅局限于文学方面，否则它也就不能真正地促使欧洲的"中国热"达

For example, such dramas performed on stage as *The Chinese Back to China*, *The Courteous Chinese*, *The Chinese*, *Chinese Gossipy Women* and *Arlequin in China* were stories using China as the background and presenting Chinese elements.

The influence of *The Orphan of Zhao* in Europe is not only limited to the literary field. Otherwise it could not have really pushed the "China fever" in Europe to a climax.

Its appeal was also manifested in its influence on European landscape architecture. From 1740 to 1786, King of Prussia Friedrich Wilhelm II issued an order to build a summer palace for short stays between the forest and lake in Potsdam and he required a hexagonal pavilion and pagoda be added to the palace. These structures were built entirely in imitation of the Chinese architectural features. He named the pavilion the "Chinese Tea Pavilion" and the pagoda "Dragon Home." The Qiuyuan Confucian Temple was built in Britain in 1745 entirely in imitation of the Confucian Temple in China and with a distinct Chinese style. The Qiuyuan Confucian Temple is an octagonal building, composed of open lattice walls and topped with a pagoda top with a bell hanged from it and a dragon bestriding it. Such a structure is characteristic of China and fully embodies Chinese people's aesthetic idea. Thanks to the appeal of *The Orphan of Zhao*, Europeans

到顶峰了。

　　它的魅力还表现在对欧洲人园林建筑方面的影响。在1740年至1786年，普鲁士国王弗里德里希·威廉二世下令，要在波茨坦的森林湖泊之间修建一座夏季行宫，他要求在这座行宫增加六角形的亭子和宝塔等建筑物，这些建筑物完全是模拟中国的建筑特色建造。他把亭子命名为"中国茶亭"，把宝塔命名为"龙之家"。英国在1745年，建造了丘园孔庙，完全仿照中国的孔庙，具有鲜明的中国风格。丘园孔庙为八角形建筑，由敞开的格构式墙组成，顶部是宝塔顶，吊着铃铛，跨着一条龙。这种构造，只有在中国才能看到，也完全体现着中国的审美思想。这种典型的中国趣味，让欧洲人在《赵氏孤儿》魅力的映照下，更感觉到趣味盎然。

　　《赵氏孤儿》在欧洲的魅力，还影响到了欧洲人的日常生活。如在法国，他们总是想方

伦敦丘园中的高塔，该塔完全以中国广州塔为模型。
Pagoda in Kew Garden, London, an imitation of a pagoda in Guangdong.

found such typical Chinese things all the more interesting.

The appeal of *The Orphan of Zhao* in Europe also made an impact on Europeans' daily life. For example, French people always tried to link things in their daily life to China. In some places in Paris and Lyon, they called public baths "Chinese baths" and a kind of playground the "Chinese maze." What's more, they called a coffee shop the "Chinese coffee shop" as all waiters in it wore Chinese costumes and there was a model of a Chinese soldier beside the staircase. It can be seen from these that the Europeans got to know more about China from *The Orphan of Zhao* popular on stage and tried every means to have such Chinese elements penetrate into every corner in

1790年，荷兰东印度公司商务官员斯赫伦堡在巴伦建立起"中国园林"，这是其中的"广州阁"，阁楼预先在广州订制，然后用商船分散装运到荷兰再行组装。
In 1790, R. Scherenbeng, a commercial official of the Dutch East India Company, built a "Chinese garden" in Baarn. The image is "Canton Pavilion," which was ordered and made in Guangzhou beforehand and shipped in separate parts to the Netherlands and then assembled.

西方人笔下的中国私家园林
Chinese private garden under westerner's description.

设法把日常生活中的一些东西，与中国挂起钩来。在巴黎和鲁昂的一些地方，他们把公共浴堂叫做"中国澡堂"，把一种游戏场所叫做"中国迷宫"。更有甚者，还把一家咖啡馆叫做"中国咖啡馆"，咖啡馆内的侍者都穿着中国服装，楼梯旁还摆放着一个中国士兵的模型。从这些可以看出，欧洲人从舞台上风行的《赵氏孤儿》，了解到了更多的中国趣味，想方设法地把这种中国风情，渗透到日常的各个生活角落。

描绘18世纪欧洲上层人士生活的绘画，集中展现了当时的"中国热"，包括中国丝绸、中国瓷器、中国茶等。
A painting describing the life of upper class in the 18th century in Europe, incarnating "China fever," including Chinese silk, porcelain, tea, etc.

their daily life.

French King Louis XV also liked "made in China" very much, especially after he read *The Orphan of China* by Voltaire, which enhanced his interest in China all the more. Certainly his interest in China as a king was different from that of ordinary people. He found some Chinese policies and measures for administering the country in *The Orphan of China* and thought they were interesting. Driven by

法国国王路易十五,也非常地喜欢"中国制造",特别是他观看了伏尔泰的《中国孤儿》后,对于中国的兴趣就更加浓厚了。当然,国王在对中国的兴趣,是与一般人不同的。他从《中国孤儿》中,看到了中国治理国家的一些政策与措施,觉得这些方法比较有意思。他在好奇心的驱使下,开始想了解更多的中国信息。当他听说,中国是一个农业大国,每年春天,中国的皇帝都要举行祭祀土地的仪式,皇帝亲自扶着犁头,做出要耕地的样子。这让他感到太有趣了,于是在1756年的春天,他就昭告全国,说他要举行祭地仪式,祈求全国今年有个好收成。他完全仿照中国皇帝祭祀大地的样子,过了一把中国皇帝祭祀的瘾。这让法国,乃至整个欧洲都轰动了。

在他的带动下,几乎所有的法国人都喜欢看《中国孤儿》,都喜欢《赵氏孤儿》的故事。并且,他们把这种从剧作和剧场里体会到的中国趣味,在国王的

法国国王路易十五像
A portrait of French King Louis XV.

curiosity, he wanted to learn more about China. He heard China was a big agricultural country and the Chinese emperor held a ceremony to worship the land every spring. The emperor held the plowshare personally and pretended to plow the land. Louis XV was very interested and declared publicly to the whole nation in the spring of 1756 that he would hold a ceremony to worship the land and pray for a good harvest that year for the country. He worshiped the land entirely in imitation of the Chinese emperor and had the fun of worshiping like a Chinese emperor. This caused a sensation in France and even the whole Europe.

Led by him, almost all the French liked reading *The Orphan of China* and liked this story. And they developed the Chinese interest they felt in the play and performance to the extreme under the leadership of the king. They always wanted to get some Chinese articles like porcelains and screens, and put them in their rooms to show a kind of Chinese flavor. They thought their status would be lowered and they would appear poorly educated and unfashionable without these Chinese articles.

From 1757 to 1759, a building was put up in Naples, Italy and it was named the "Chinese Room." All the walls and ceilings of the room were built with ceramic tiles made in China and the indoor flowery decorations were embossed and painted with the typical Chinese patterns

18世纪销往欧洲的中国瓷器，瓷器上的绘画表现了当时欧洲商人在中国订购茶叶的情景。
Porcelain sold to Europe in the 18th century, the painting on which showed the European businessman buying tea in China.

带领下，发展到了极致。他们总是想弄到一些中国的物品，如瓷器、屏风等等，将其摆放在房间里，显示一种中国情调。好像没有这些中国物品，他们的身份就会大大降低，他们就会显得没有文化、不解时尚。在1757至1759年，意大利的那不勒斯建造了一座建筑物，它被命名为"中国房间"。这个房间的墙壁和天花板都是用中国制造的瓷砖镶砌而成，室内的花饰呈浮雕状，画有鸟、蝴蝶、龙等中国房间布置的典型图

like birds, butterflies and dragons. After he saw the room, the king of Spain ordered his minister to build an identical "Chinese Room." It can be seen how things with Chinese flavor had fascinated Europeans thanks to the appeal of *The Orphan of Zhao*.

Macartney, a famous British diplomatist, recorded such a phenomenon in his diary. He wrote the following paragraph when he recorded the European society in 1792 in his diary: "The whole Europe is fascinated with China. Decorative cloth is hung in palaces like grocery stores in the heaven. Genuine pieces cost so much that people have to resort to replications." It can be seen that what he saw was a general social phenomenon in the then Europe. Such a phenomenon was just attributable to the appeal of Chinese culture transmitted by *The Orphan of Zhao*.

画。西班牙国王看过这个房间后，就命令大臣，要想办法也建造一个一模一样的"中国房间"。可见，在《赵氏孤儿》魅力的影射下，中国趣味的东西是多么地让欧洲人着迷。

对于这种现象，英国著名外交官马嘎尔尼曾在他的日记中有所记录。他在日记中记录1792年的欧洲现象时，他写了这样一段话："整个欧洲都对中国着了迷。那里的宫殿里挂着中国图案的装饰布，就像天朝的杂货铺。真货价值千金，于是只好仿造。"可见，他所描述的是当时欧洲一种普遍的社会现象，这种欧洲普遍流行的现象，正是《赵氏孤儿》传播的中国文化魅力所致。

Classic dramatic view

The imitation of the ancient Greek and Roman art forms was advocated in art in Europe from the 17th century to the end of the 18th century, that is to respect traditions, advocate rationality, pursue the balanced and concise style and use elegant and standard national languages. This artistic proposition is called classicism. Afterwards it was replaced by romanticism which emerged in the 19th century.

A dramatic school was developed under the influence of the classic aesthetic theory. It was established in France between the 1630s and 1670s. In 1638, Sharplan (1595–1674), one of the founders of L'Institut de France, wrote Opinions of L'Institut de France on Le cid, saying that Corneille violated the "amusement" role of dramas "based on rationality," failed to give priority to "satisfying the requirement of honor" and to observe the "Three Unities." In 1674, Boileau, another academician of L'Institut de France, published *Art of Poetry*, which marked the official formation of the classic dramatic theory.

The main characteristics of the classic dramatic view are as follows: it advocates royalty and exhibits a distinct political tendency in politics, advocates rationality and despises sexual passion in expression of feelings, regards ancient Greek and Roman dramas as models in the creation of works, emphasizes regularity in dramatic structure and especially the "Three Unities" in the creation of drama, and pays attention to accuracy, elegance and logic in drama language; actors should express feelings of their roles according to the set program, and symmetry, vanity and tranquility are pursued on stage.

In the 19th century, with the impact of romanticism on classicism, the romantic dramatic view began to take the lead and replaced the classic dramatic view.

古典主义戏剧观

在17世纪至18世纪末的欧洲，在艺术上主张模仿古希腊、罗马的艺术形式，尊重传统，崇尚理性，追求均衡、简洁的风格，使用典雅的民族规范语言。这种艺术主张被称为古典主义，后来被19世纪兴起的浪漫主义代替。

在古典主义美学理论的影响下，形成了一种戏剧流派，这个流派的确立是在17世纪30至70年代的法国。1638年，法兰西学院创始人之一沙波兰撰写了《法兰西学院对〈熙德〉的意见书》一文，指责高乃依违背了戏剧"以理性为根据"的"娱乐"作用，没有始终把"满足荣誉的要求"放在首位，未能严格遵守"三一律"等。到1674年，另一位法兰西学院院士布瓦洛发表的《诗的艺术》，标志着古典主义戏剧理论的正式形成。

古典主义戏剧观的主要特征是：在政治上拥护王权，表现出鲜明的政治倾向性；在情感表述上崇尚理性，蔑视情欲；在作品创作上奉古希腊、罗马的戏剧为典范；在戏剧结构十分强调规范化，特别强调戏剧创作要遵循"三一律"，戏剧语言要讲究准确、高雅、合乎逻辑，演员要按规定的程式来表现角色的感情，舞台场面追求对称、浮华和宁静。

到19世纪，随着浪漫主义对古典主义的冲击，浪漫主义戏剧观开始走向主导地位，代替了古典主义戏剧观。